Have invisible entities controlled the destiny of mankind?

By **DAVID BRYANT**

UNINVITED COMPANIONS

Copyright © 2015 David Bryant. All rights reserved.

First paperback edition printed 2015 in the United Kingdom.

A catalogue record for this book is available from the British Library.

ISBN 978-0-9574944-7-3

No part of this book shall be reproduced or transmitted in any form or by any means, electronic or mechanical, including photocopying, recording, or by any information retrieval system without written permission of the publisher.

Published by

Heathland Books

For more copies of this book, please email: info@spacerocksuk.com

Telephone: 01603 715933

Designed and typeset by Bob Tibbitts ~ (iSET)

Printed in Great Britain

Although every precaution has been taken in the preparation of this book, the publisher and author assume no responsibility for errors or omissions. Neither is any liability assumed for damages resulting from the use of this information contained within.

"There are more things in heaven and earth, Horatio,
             than are dreamt of in your philosophy."

William Shakespeare, *Hamlet*

Contents

Acknowledgements 7

Foreword by the Rev R L Fanthorpe 9

Introduction 11

Chapter One: **Encounters** 17

Chapter Two: **Get out the duster!** 27

Chapter Three: **Things that *don't* go bump in the night!** 33

Chapter Four: **Searching for a pattern** 43

Chapter Five: **Elemental, my dear Watson!** 53

Chapter Six: **Wormholes, portals and interdimensional highways!** .. 61

Chapter Seven: **Paranormal entities: are they *alive*?** 71

Chapter Eight: **Energy beings: the destiny of intelligent life?** .. 77

Chapter Nine: **Towards an understanding** 85

Chapter Ten: **If God did not exist, we would have to invent him** 93

Chapter Eleven:	**Can parascience ever become a science?**	99
Chapter Twelve:	**Uninvited companions**	107
Appendix One:	**Around and about in Rendlesham Forest**	121
Appendix Two:	**Abductions in theory and practice**	127
Appendix Three:	**A circular argument!**	133
Appendix Four:	**Can Energy Beings control our behaviour?**	137
Appendix Five:	**"Play up! play up! and play the game!"**	141
Appendix Six:	**Images of the paranormal**	145
Glossary		153
Bibliography		159
Picture credits		161

ACKNOWLEDGEMENTS

WRITING a book isn't as hard as you might imagine: in my case I can be quite productive, provided I have certain pre-requisites in place:

- Somewhere quiet to work.
- An outline of what I want to write.
- A long-suffering wife who understands when I get up at four in the morning because I've woken up with a new thought buzzing around in my head that I just *have* to get down on paper.
- An editor and publisher who both know how to say the right things to keep me going to the end.
- A bottle of decent Burgundy to celebrate when I've managed to get an idea across in the way I intended.
- A strong index finger on my right hand (I can't type!)

So firstly, I'd like to express my gratitude to my business partner, best friend and love of my life, Linda: every idea I ever have is presented to her before anyone else gets to hear about it!

I must also say thanks to Rev. R Lionel Fanthorpe, not just for agreeing to write a foreword, but also for showing me over forty years ago that **"The Universe is not only stranger than we imagine, it's stranger than we <u>can</u> imagine!"** He chatted to me about the mysteries of Rennes-le-Chateau many

UNINVITED COMPANIONS

years before it became fashionable (and profitable!) to do so and encouraged me to write my first book about the paranormal!

Bob Tibbitts, my editor, designer and typesetter, is the most patient, accommodating person you could wish for: he accepts my modifications with good-humour and resignation and is entirely responsible for the final appearance of my output. Cheers Bob!

Thanks to the viticulturalists of the *Saône* region and, to a lesser extent, those of Bordeaux: what would we have to drink with cheese, good bread and olives without you all!

Finally: my gratitude to you for buying this book. (Assuming you did buy it, not borrow it from a friend or find it on a park bench somewhere!) No author has the right to assume he has an audience that will share his enthusiasms: thanks for sharing mine!

FOREWORD

By LIONEL FANTHORPE

DAVID Bryant and I were teaching colleagues at Hellesdon High School, near Norwich over forty years ago. David was a particularly gifted science teacher, and pupils always responded enthusiastically to his logical, rational and analytical approach to the subject – especially when he was introducing an area of the curriculum that was new to them, and from their perspective something of an unsolved mystery. As friends and professional colleagues, David and I did not take long to discover that we had a shared interest in paranormal phenomena and an objective approach to it. This approach is widely shared by members of ASSAP (The Association for the Scientific Study of Anomalous Phenomena) of which I have the honour of being President, and my wife Patricia is their First Lady.

There are three very important aspects to David's latest book. The first is his admirable approach to the topic; the second is his choice of subject; the third is his very fluent and lucid writing style which makes the book a genuine pleasure to read.

He embraces a wide range of paranormal phenomena in the book and links them effectively to the central topic: the mysterious orbs that are currently attracting so much serious scientific attention. Investigators are hypothesising widely about their nature. Departed human spirits? Extraterrestrial aliens? Paranormal entities such as angels, djinn or demons? Unusual forms of energy? Observational aberrations? Might some reports of orbs fall into one of those categories while others have totally different explanations?

The orb phenomena raise the question about the mysterious nature of self-awareness and intelligence. Many years ago, I had an interesting discussion with a friend who theorised that the sun was inhabited by flame giants who were highly intelligent and self-aware. If mind can exist independently of physical matter – and there is a significant amount of evidence to suggest that it can – then does that add an important philosophical dimension to the quest for the truth about orbs?

There is also the age old question of the relationship between an individual human being and his, or her, environment. While the traditional butcher, baker and candlestick-maker are making things – *the things that they make are making them.* The very act of contributing to the environment means that the environment is contributing something to us. The very act of observing the environment means that the observations we make are also making us. When we observe the mysterious orb phenomenon, it is having an effect on us. Confrontation with the unexplained has an inevitable impact on the human mind, and this is where David's book is so valuable: his careful, rational examination of the orb phenomenon enables the reader to join in that logical investigation.

Investigating strange phenomena like the orbs also makes a worthwhile contribution to scientific progress. It is by investigating and researching the unknown that we unravel important new knowledge. If they turn out to be some strange new form of energy, perhaps that energy can be harnessed and utilised in ways that will do good in the future.

INTRODUCTION

THIS book is an examination of the paranormal phenomena known as Orbs: the strange spheres of light that frequently appear on video and still photographs or are even, at times, seen by the unaided eye.

I should say straight away that **without doubt**, many of the images captured by digital cameras actually show dust, mist or fine raindrops: but not all!

The book will examine many apparently unrelated paranormal phenomena and consider whether they might be linked in some way: an attempt to construct a kind of 'Unified Paranormal Theory'!

But before we throw ourselves in at the deep end, I'd better start by confessing that, like the UFO phenomenon, I had already begun to form an opinion about orbs when I was quite young. To understand how this came about, and how subsequent experiences led to the central thesis of the book, I must, I'm afraid, share with you a few autobiographical details.

I occasionally reflect on how lucky I was to have been born in 1951, just a few years after the end of the Second World War. It's true that some foods and luxury items were still rationed and that large areas of the East End of London, where I grew up, still bore the scars of the German Blitz, but it was a period when most people shared a great optimism about the future.

Britain's industrial centres had been devastated by bombing and many skilled workers had been killed in the fighting, but *mater artium necessitas*,

UNINVITED COMPANIONS

as the Romans apparently used to say. Using technologies acquired during the war, the British aerospace industry flourished in the 1950s: the de Havilland Comet became the world's first jet airliner and the sky began to be criss-crossed with the contrails of the RAF's high-performance fighter and bomber aircraft. Television and radio were finally both within the reach of normal families (even though it would be ingenuous to pretend that Hopalong Cassidy and Prudence the Kitten were worth the wait!) I vividly remember the difference a washing machine and refrigerator made to my mother's life: for me, the fact that milk didn't taste revolting after just two days was reason enough to celebrate!

At the time, school children in their final year of primary school sat an examination known as the 'Eleven Plus'. Those who achieved the lowest marks went on to Secondary Modern Schools: despite acquiring a bad name in the seventies, these – and the Technical Schools that middle-band students attended – provided a disciplined and productive five-year preparation for life in the adult world. (My first post in Education was teaching Agriculture and Rural Studies at a Secondary Modern in Norfolk: the happiest years of my career!)

As it happens, firstly my brother Rob, and then I passed the 11+ and moved on to Grammar School. After an initial three years grounding in the classics, modern languages, the humanities and science, students were divided by interest and aptitude into two cohorts: Arts and Sciences. Although the expectation was that Grammar School leavers would go on to University, I think the idea was that one group would ultimately move towards banking, insurance, the Civil Service and the arts, while the others would become captains of industry, engineers and military officers. (Actually, in the 60s, I reckon a fair percentage went into teaching or pop music!)

For my brother and me, there was no contest: he 'opted' for Science in Year 10 and, despite a leaning towards rebellion and the guitar, I did the

UNINVITED COMPANIONS

same two years later. Our study groups were comprised entirely of embryonic boffins and our teachers treated us as such! We used to swan about in white lab coats most of the day and were encouraged to think of ourselves as members of an intellectual elite!

When my brother was about thirteen, he and a group of friends became very interested in a genre of popular writing known as Science Fiction. This had its beginnings in the United States with popular pocket-sized magazines such as **'Amazing Stories'**, **'Galaxy'**, **'If'** and **'Astounding'**. These are generally referred to as pulp fiction, because they were printed on rough, low-quality paper made from wood pulp. They had several things in common: they had well-crafted, full-colour covers (often, to our delight, featuring semi-naked women!), short, thought-provoking stories based around future-science themes such as space and time travel, and they could be bought with the average weekly pocket money of 2/- (That's 10p to most of you!) Every week, Rob and his friends would each buy a different one and pass them around the group!

I can still remember my first exposure to these pocket treasures: I was 10, in hospital (having had my tonsils removed) and bored. One visiting hour, my mother (suddenly realising that chocolates weren't such a great idea) went off to the WI shop and returned with half a dozen titles: I imagine she'd recognised the cover of one she'd seen in my brother's bedroom. I was hooked . . .

From these, we rapidly graduated to paperback books. Again: these were a bit of a novelty at the time: cheap, easily available and with new titles appearing continually. My favourites were those published by **Badger Books**: I built up a collection of hundreds of them! At some point I noticed that the names of many of the authors – Bron Fane, Trebor Thorpe, Pel Torro, Oben Leterth, Elton T Neef and Peter O'Flinn were partial anagrams of each other! Years later (when I was teaching agriculture) I discovered

UNINVITED COMPANIONS

that the Deputy Headmaster – to whom I had confessed a taste for Science Fiction – was none-other than Robert Lionel Fanthorpe, the author of all those books! His *noms de plume* were constructed from random letters from his name! He wrote over 180 books for Badger and plenty more besides: since we taught and attended the Norwich Science Fiction Club together, he's become a Clergyman, author of many paranormal books and TV pundit!

One of my favourite SF authors then – and now – was Eric Frank Russell. His books are often amusing, frequently disturbing and always thought provoking. One of the very first I read was **'Sinister Barrier'**, first published in an American magazine in 1939: I bought the 1966 paperback edition from Bob Sherry's bookstall on Romford Market and have occasionally wished I hadn't! I'm not going to give the whole plot away: find a copy and read it! But in essence, the story revolves around the discovery that humans are basically the prey-animal of invisible, spherical entities. Invisible, that is, until one of the characters, Professor Bjornsen, discovers a formula to extend the range of human eyesight. As Russell writes in the novel:

"The scale of electro-magnetic vibrations extends over sixty octaves, of which the human eye can see but one. Beyond that sinister barrier of our limitations, outside that poor, ineffective range of vision, bossing every man jack of us from the cradle to the grave, invisibly preying on us as ruthlessly as any parasite, are our malicious, all-powerful lords and masters – the creatures who really own the Earth!"

Even as a kid, this was not a comfortable thought! How much less so when my strange Jack Kerouac-like Uncle John (a proto-Hippie who eventually 'tuned in and dropped out' on the west coast of the USA) encouraged me to develop my own senses through meditation and aura-discerning exercises. I occasionally began to glimpse translucent orbs just like those in Russell's book, beginning a quest for evidence of these elusive entities that has lasted for 50 years.

UNINVITED COMPANIONS

Advance warning! This account will, I'm afraid, include a few autobiographical memories: I honestly believe that their inclusion will add something to your enjoyment of the book and understanding of its subject: I hope you agree!

CHAPTER ONE

ENCOUNTERS

I RECKON that these days most people have heard of orbs or even seen them on television: there has been a succession of TV programs since the mid-noughties featuring groups of more or less hysterical 'Ghost Researchers' chasing around reputedly haunted locations with expensive EMF meters, infra-red cameras and voice boxes. At best these have been credible and entertaining, particularly the one where the two leading investigators are ghost hunters at night and plumbers during the daytime. But at worst, some other programs have done a lot to raise general levels of scepticism, not the least when participants are seen covertly chucking stones and cutlery about!

Most of these programs have at one time or another captured fast-moving, apparently self-luminous balls moving through camera shot. To their credit, the presenters often immediately identify the objects as dust particles or insects, but occasionally (and correctly, IMHO) they identify these as authentically paranormal phenomena.

We should, I suppose define 'paranormal' at this stage! The latin prefix *para* means 'outside' or 'beyond': thus paranormal means 'that which is outside or beyond the normal' (Of course, what is normal for you and me might be different from what was normal for, say, Aleister Crowley!)

UNINVITED COMPANIONS

Orbs, by this definition, are self-guided translucent spheres that cannot currently be explained in terms of known scientific principles: once a credible explanation is found, of course, they will no longer be paranormal! Familiar examples of this are rainbows, comets and eclipses: to our ancestors, these were mystical and inexplicable and inspired all kinds of mythology. Despite the undoubted fascination of a total solar eclipse, it's not as awe-inspiring now we know it isn't the result of the Sun being devoured by a dragon!

UNINVITED COMPANIONS

I am absolutely certain that much of today's parascience would, if carefully investigated, eventually be accepted into mainstream science. Mind you, that's a big 'if' given the conservative nature of science!

But there are plenty of precedents: continental drift, the Giant Squid and black holes come to mind.

Let me pose a question! Do you occasionally watch the TV or read in a dimly-lit room? This might be illuminated by side lights or even by just the television screen. If so, have you ever noticed a moving object in the corner of your vision: something that was seemed real, yet which disappeared as you glanced across for closer scrutiny? I became aware of this phenomenon when I was quite young: when I mentioned it to others it was always dismissed as 'A trick of the light' or some such catch-all explanation. Until, that is, I mentioned it to my Uncle John, the proto-hippie!

To my delight (and surprise) he wasn't at all sceptical: in fact, he suggested strategies to develop my ability to see these objects with greater clarity. (Without going into detail, these involved sitting in a darkened room, touching the finger tips of my hands together and looking sideways at them as I gradually drew them apart. (Try it yourself: it *can* produce instant results for those with open minds!)

This procedure seemed to 'tune up' my peripheral vision and, quite quickly, I found I could resolve the almost subliminal moving objects that drifted across the carpet into pearl-lustred, almost opalescent spheres: orbs, in fact! Once I could see these fascinating objects, I found they would turn up almost anywhere (although I never observed one in broad daylight until a very disturbing encounter that took place many years later)

Having passed through the education system, joined the Navy and (thanks to a spell of pneumonia at just the wrong time) returned abruptly to civilian life, I decided to give teaching a bash! I applied to Brentwood College

UNINVITED COMPANIONS

of Education (now incorporated into Anglia Ruskin University). Although the Cert Ed course was quite rigorous and seemingly designed to generate stereotypic teachers, I soon found a group of 'freaks to hang with'. I spent a delightful three years surrounded by kaftans, long hair, Indian music and exotic-smelling cigarettes! Chief 'freak' was John Power, who was very much our guru: he went on to become a celebrated writer, lecturer, orientalist and artist. Nearly fifty years later I remain in contact with him, and with another profound influence: Graeme Douglas. He was part of a clique of innovative musicians that were to coalesce into bands such as the Kursaal Flyers, Eddy & the Hot Rods and Dr Feelgood. Great days!

Going from the rigid discipline of BRNC Dartmouth to the liberation of student life – and membership of a social group that shared a total acceptance of the arcane and occult – helped me develop the ability to see orbs and auras without really trying. (I wonder to what extent our early conditioning by parents, peers, school and society destroys an innate ability in this area?)

Despite throwing myself into the worlds of astronomy, education, meteoritics and online commerce, I'm still an old hippy at heart and have never lost an interest in paranormal phenomena, nor the ability to witness many of its intriguing aspects.

Quite a long time ago, I started to think more deeply about orbs. I suppose I'd just taken them for granted without really considering what they might be! The conclusions I reached were:

Orbs are an authentic, repeatable phenomenon, seen and photographed by many ordinary people: they often appear in images on social networking sites, for example.

There is only one type of 'genuine' orb: although they may vary in size, transparency, colour and contents!

UNINVITED COMPANIONS

Some orbs seem to respond to human attempts at communication.

Under certain circumstances, vast clusters of orbs can rapidly appear.

I suppose the biggest contribution to the library of photographic images available to a modern researcher (and the largest source of deliberate fakes!) is the digital camera. Not that many years ago, no-one would wander around a wood at night, randomly taking picture after picture if all the films had to be taken into the chemists for development and printing: it would've cost a fortune and could be a little haphazard at times!

I remember leaving two rolls of film at a well-known high street shop for processing. These were images (on high ASA film) of Comet West, which put in such a spectacular appearance in 1976 that many people consider it a Great Comet. When I returned to collect my prints, I was given two new films and a letter of apology from the branch manager, saying that the films had been ruined during development, so that 'just a few streaks appeared on the negatives.'

With digicams and modern SLRs, an investigator can take literally thousands of pictures, stored on SD cards with capacities up to 512GB at the time of writing! At home, these can be downloaded onto a PC and, with software such as Irfanview or Paintshop, rapidly checked for interesting or anomalous content. There is a strange irony in the circular argument one often encounters in regard to photographic evidence of the paranormal, It goes:

"With everyone having a phone camera or digicam, why aren't there any decent pictures of UFOs?"

"There are! Here's a website full of them! And videos!"

"Huh! They're <u>too</u> good: they must be fakes!"

Some years ago my wife Linda and I both bought inexpensive digital

UNINVITED COMPANIONS

cameras: hers a Nikon, mine a Canon. These were small enough to slip into a pocket and had 2GB SD cards: we used them for (among other things) photographing scenes of paranormal and supernatural happenings to use on our '**Chilling Tales UK**' website. (This has been online since the nineties, one of the oldest such websites in the UK!)

Inevitably, we began to capture images of orbs. At times it seemed as if they appeared out of a sense of curiosity in what we were up to: they would arrive in twos and threes until finally the images were crowded with them!

Some locations (particularly the Rendlesham Forest) seemed particularly attractive to orbs: regardless of the weather and time of year, as long as it was dark enough, they began to appear in our photographs: sometimes they were visible to the naked eye.

This would be the ideal place to dispel two popular myths about orbs (and the vapours and mists which are often associated with them) Orbs are not out-of-focus images of dust particles, rain drops or insects! Some of

UNINVITED COMPANIONS

UNINVITED COMPANIONS

the most impressive photos we have taken were on dry, moonless, frosty nights in the forest, when the paths are frozen solid and not a single insect is on the wing. At other times, in other places, we have taken images where raindrops, insects and even bats are clearly discernible for what they are. Moreover, genuine orbs appear on our photographs in a range of colours and textures: I really can't imagine a mechanism by which this could be the case with raindrops or dust! (Actually, Rendlesham Forest is not generally a dusty place: the main tracks are sandy, often with a thatch of short grass.)

Sometimes we have actually witnessed orbs forming or condensing from patches of mist: we have even captured this on camera a couple of times. On one amazing occasion in broad daylight I photographed two huge orbs that were apparently connected by a long, parallel-sided tube: the whole formation twisted and writhed like a snake!

UNINVITED COMPANIONS

In December, 2010 Linda, several friends and I attended a UFO conference at Woodbridge, Suffolk. This was the 30th anniversary of the Bentwaters / Rendlesham Forest Incident, which I intended to document in my **'Chilling Tales UK'** website. Accordingly, we spent some time in the forest before the event, photographing the various locations discussed in their presentations by witnesses Jim Penniston, John Burroughs and Larry Warren. It grew dark quite early and Linda was keen to try to photograph orbs and mists – phenomena we had witnessed on previous visits – before we needed to return to Woodbridge for the conference. Our focus was the notorious Track 10, which has reputedly had more than its fair share of paranormal activity. It was here in August the same year that a group of us witnessed a fifty-centimetre metallic-green orb cross the path ten metres ahead.

You may well be thinking "I thought Rendlesham Forest was all about UFOs, not paranormal goings-on!" And I can't argue with you, because the same thought occurred to me when I first met author Brenda Butler and her niece Beverley there. As we walked through the dark forest together, she would occasionally describe previous bizarre sightings the pair had experienced together:

"Here's where we saw the Yeti!" or *"That's where you often see pumas!"*

I must confess that Brenda's perfectly earnest accounts of the many strange things she and Beverley had witnessed did initially bring out the sceptic in me, but I logged the information for future consideration: some of what she has told me has informed parts of this book. One thing that Beverley told us has turned out to be surprisingly useful: as we stood quietly on Track 10, she whispered to us that orbs are sometimes attracted if you whistle! Accordingly, Linda gave it a try: whistling softly, she took a succession of photos with her digicam. We huddled together to examine the results on the camera's small preview screen. To our surprise, Beverley's advice seemed to have worked! Each successive image held more and brighter orbs . . .

UNINVITED COMPANIONS

So, to the initial list of 'orb characteristics' I will add a couple more

Orbs seem to appear most frequently around sites associated with other paranormal activity.

Orbs seem to almost 'feed off' human excitement, growing bigger and brighter in the process!

So what, then, might they be? Let us briefly review all the possibilities that have occurred to me (and to other researchers) and then examine them in greater detail, devoting a section to each:

- Orbs are photographic artefacts or caused by defects of vision.

- Orbs are spirit-entities: ghosts of dead humans not yet capable of full-body manifestation.

- Orbs are some form of elemental spirit, in the same broad category as elves, fairies, nymphs, etc.

- Orbs are vehicles or devices which enable entities from other realities, times or parallel universes to visit our world.

- Orbs are an invisible life-form that has shared our planet for millennia and interact with us for their own purposes.

CHAPTER TWO

GET OUT THE DUSTER!

It is undeniable that smudges on your camera lens, shutter or sensor can, under the right circumstances, produce images that resemble 'authentic' orbs. Small insects, raindrops and dust particles are undoubtedly all factors too.

The first of these can easily be discounted, because dirt on your camera will not only stay the same size and appear in exactly the same place in each photo you take in a sequence, but will continue to do so until you get the lens cloth out!

Insects are a little more difficult to dismiss. It's surprising just how many flying insects are out there: believe it or not, the best estimates (based on aerial sampling) suggest that three billion pass over your head every month! That's over **four million** per hour! Of course, many of these are extremely high and wouldn't show up in your photos, but plenty occupy the same airspace as we do!

One of my interests – well: passions, to be honest! – is wildlife photography. On a fair percentage of my bird pictures gnats and small flies can be seen stooging across the frame. If they are closer to the camera than the bird, they can appear as little fuzzy spheres. At night, using a flash of

UNINVITED COMPANIONS

any sort, they resemble snowballs! But – and here's the crunch – unless they are very small, they are always brilliantly white and dense and frequently display some evidence of wings, legs or antennae.

Furthermore, you'd expect to see many more 'orbs' on photos taken where insects are visibly abundant, like marshes or heathland. In fact I have taken hundreds of pictures of crepuscular birds in such places and that simply hasn't been the case.

Flash photograph of a Nightjar taken on a July evening when the air was *alive* with midges: none appear in the picture!

Some types of raindrop, however, really can look like 'the real thing': not the heavy drops that fall during a proper rain shower, but the persistent 'mizzle' that quickly soaks anyone caught out in it. They can appear on

UNINVITED COMPANIONS

Bentwaters UFO witnesses John Burroughs and Jim Penniston with friend and fellow-researcher Paul Williams: we knew it was raining and noticed the 'orbs' straight away!

photographs as translucent spheres of different sizes, depending on their distance from the camera (See the episode of 'Father Ted' with Dougal and the Cows for a full explanation!) But there are a couple of factors that eliminate raindrops as the origin of many orb images: firstly, I'm not in the habit of taking photographs in the rain – particularly not with my wildlife set up, which cost quite a few hundred pounds – and I would suspect that's true of the majority of photographers. More obviously, most of us tend to notice when it's raining! It is my recollection that every one of the orb images in this book that purport to have a paranormal origin was taken on a completely dry evening, either on cold and frosty winter expeditions, or late at night after warm summer days: I'm no masochist!

It is undeniable that flash photographs taken on misty nights can **occasionally** display some or all of the phenomena that we are considering. I've tried this, and the result will generally be a semi-opaque veil in front of the subject of the picture, with large numbers of bright 'orbs'. I have certainly

UNINVITED COMPANIONS

been shown a number of such images by enthusiasts, but it is always obvious how they were obtained.

As I stated right at the start of this book, it is undeniable that many of the images of orbs we see in books or on popular TV series are, in fact, dust particles. Most of the ghost hunting programmes are filmed in old, often derelict buildings, tunnels and caves, and it would be unrealistic to suppose that motes disturbed by the presenters and film crews don't get misinterpreted in stills images. But how about moving orbs in video clips? These, too can be produced when air movements from open doors and windows cause dust to drift around the shot. Not infrequently, though, apparently genuine orbs appear, move across the screen quite rapidly and disappear by seemingly passing through a solid wall: these, I would argue, are the real deal. As with all paranormal phenomena, even if you **can** explain 99.9% of records, that still leaves a heck of a lot that you **can't!**

As before: most of my images in this book were taken in locations where there just wasn't any dust...

We are probably all familiar with the small, transparent shapes that appear to drift in front of our eyes when we look up at a bright sky. These have two usual causes: most frequent are posterior vitreous detachments or PVDs. These are small fragments of jelly-like vitreous humour (the clear gel that fills the space between the eye's lens and the retina) As we grow older, this can become more liquid, allowing thicker pieces to detach and drift about: their shadows on the retina are responsible for most of the floating spots we see. Another source of these is the fine capillaries that carry blood across the conjunctiva at the front of the eye. This thin, transparent membrane is alive and, like all living tissue, needs oxygen and 'food' to survive: this it receives from its own blood supply. Against a bright background, it is possible to see these hair-thin blood vessels and the *rouleaux* of erythrocytes inside them. Although these are undoubtedly responsible for some eye-witness accounts

UNINVITED COMPANIONS

of daylight discs, orbs and flying entities, these, of course, could not appear on a photograph.

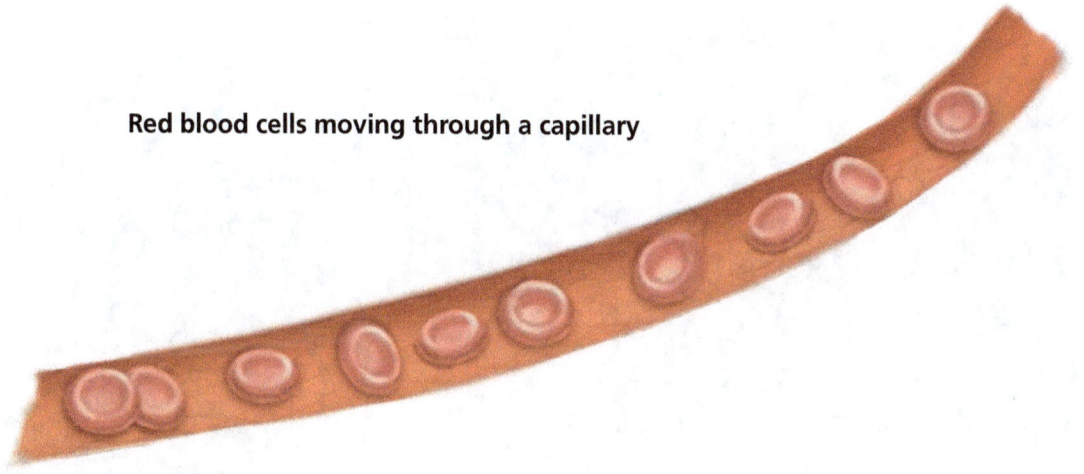

Red blood cells moving through a capillary

UNINVITED COMPANIONS

Coalescing mist and orbs, Track 10, Rendlesham Forest

CHAPTER THREE

THINGS THAT *DON'T* GO BUMP IN THE NIGHT!

YOU'VE probably already noticed that orbs are most often seen in the media in articles and TV programmes about ghosts: could there perhaps be a link between the two phenomena?

Before we can investigate that question, we have briefly to address another, more fundamental one first: what *are* ghosts?

A full examination of this topic would fill a bookshelf, but we can at least consider the generally-agreed ideas and how they fit into our discussion of the orb phenomena.

The first thing to say is, of course, that there is no consensus as to what ghosts are or even if they exist! Considering the fact that literally millions of people claim to have seen one, it's a little surprising that scientific investigators tend to concern themselves with the psychological pathology of the witnesses. (Generally, they'll reach the conclusions that, if you claim to have seen a ghost, you are either a liar, self-deluded or nuts!) I've always found that difficult to understand, given that (apart from communist states) every country on Earth is either a theocracy or has an allegiance to some religion or another. The central core of all the major religions is a belief in some form of afterlife, whether spiritual or actual, which requires the

UNINVITED COMPANIONS

existence of the human soul. As a child, I found it quite confusing that adults would tell you that ghosts didn't exist and yet, in church services, school assemblies and RE lessons, you were told about the Christian trilogy of 'The Father, Son and the Holy Ghost'.

The generally-held view of western society is, I suppose, that ghosts are the spirits of dead people. Since, according to most religious beliefs, we are all supposed to go either to some form of heaven or hell, there has to be some suggestion as to why ghosts linger here among us. The most frequently offered theories seem to be that ghosts are:

- **The troubled spirits of people who have been murdered or wrongly-treated and who are looking for justice.**

- **The spirits of people who died so abruptly that they don't realise they are dead.**

- **The spirits of truly evil humans who wish to carry on being so after death.**

- **The spirits of caring, loving individuals who wish to act as 'guardian angels' to their grieving families.**

- **The spirits of wrong-doers or unbelievers who are being punished for their actions by being forced to live in limbo for eternity.**

- **Images in some form of 'replay' of past events, somehow recorded in an object, building or historical location.**

- **Evil spirits from hell – the antithesis of angels – that stalk the Earth to confuse, frighten or subvert humans.**

I must confess to having seen lots of apparent ghosts, usually in the company of others. These fit into most of the categories above, ranging from deceased relatives to phantom aircraft and, once, even a whole

UNINVITED COMPANIONS

army! I haven't been able to reconcile these experiences with any of the conventional scientific explanations, but I am certain that at least some of them are connected with the orb phenomenon.

I don't propose to write accounts of all my experiences with what would generally be described as ghosts, but there are a few that are relevant to our development of an ultimate conclusion.

Many years ago, during the time when I worked as a teacher with Rev Lionel Fanthorpe, I happened to mention that I had long been interested in Cryptozoology and had, in fact visited Loch Ness many times. The first was as long ago as the early sixties when the Loch Ness Investigation Board had cameras with long telephoto lenses mounted around the Loch as well as mobile rigs on Bedford vans. Another colleague called Phil – a dour brummie chemistry teacher – shared my interest and Lionel suggested we conduct a scientific investigation at the Loch and present the results in a book. Accordingly, over the following two years, I spent as much time as possible in the Great Glen – sometimes alone, sometimes with Phil – interviewing witnesses, visiting the scenes of historical sightings and conducting dawn to dusk vigils high above the northern road just east of Urquhart Castle. It was interesting, if tiring work and we met many fascinating people, from Dr Robert Rines of the Boston Academy of Science, to Prof Roy Mackal, Nicholas Witchell and Alex Campbell. There were a few bizarre encounters too: Frank Searle, an ex-marine with a false leg who lived on the Loch's stony shore in a caravan being the most entertaining.

We were there when Dr Rines obtained his famous (and largely since discredited) photographs of the monster's head and neck: this was the end of the line for our book, because Nick Witchell scooped us by obtaining rights to use the photos in his work **'The Loch Ness Story'** which was published in 1974.

UNINVITED COMPANIONS

Among the places I investigated were the shingle beach and woods where the little River Enrick empties into Urquhart Bay, and the graveyard near Boleskine House (once home to Aleister Crowley and, much later, Jimmy Page, the Led Zeppelin guitarist) Neither were ideal venues for the faint-hearted to spend the night, but I did so, taking photographs from time to time. On almost all of these, orbs could be seen (None of which were visible at the time, but only when the films were developed back home in Norfolk.) while both locations produced images of what appeared to be vaguely human-shaped mists.

Our researches at the Loch produced a thick folder of folk tales and personal accounts, a surprising number of which concerned various ghostly encounters, rather than the expected lake monster stories. These ranged from Roman Galleys to RAF bombers crashing into the Loch. (Strangely enough, a Vickers Wellington was recovered from the dark waters of Loch Ness some years later!) The whole Great Glen is a renowned UFO hotspot, and I collected many eye-witness accounts from people from a variety of backgrounds.

We had become firmly convinced that the Loch could not possibly support even a single large creature, never mind the breeding colony that would be required to account for its long history of monstrous sightings. Then, against all our expectations, we actually saw one at close range! (See CGI image!)

One afternoon we had arranged to spend a couple of hours in the company of Nick Witchell in his caravan overlooking Urquhart Bay. We were driving towards our rendezvous along the northern shore when, as we passed the village of Achnahannet, I happened to glance towards the water. To my amazement a large, living creature was sculling lazily past the John Cobb marker post on Johnnie's Point. It resembled nothing more nor less than the grey back of an elephant: I skidded my Escort Mexico into a lay-by

UNINVITED COMPANIONS

UNINVITED COMPANIONS

and Phil and I tumbled down the scree slope to the lochside. At 50 metres range, it was obvious to us both that we were watching the back of a living creature that was predating the shoals of migratory fish concentrated by the jutting peninsula of the point. The beast moved round the point before heading out to mid-loch, where it submerged with barely a ripple. After a few seconds I turned to Phil, his face a mask of incredulity. At this point I reflected upon the two cine cameras with 500 mm lenses on the back seat of the car! What an opportunity we had missed!

Since that day in 1972, I have had several encounters with the supernatural and mythical: strange to relate, whenever I have had camera equipment to hand, I have almost always either failed to use it or (more mysteriously!) it has failed to function!

It was this fact that began a train of thought that, forty years later, would result in this book: were the ghostly manifestations, the UFOs, the 'water horses', the orbs all separate aspects of a single phenomenon?

On one occasion I was asked to give a talk about UFOs to a small exclusive group that included some TV executives, gentleman landowners and a couple of airline pilots. The venue was a beautiful old Elizabethan house on the Norfolk-Suffolk border. After a buffet supper, we adjourned to a large drawing room with an inglenook fireplace: I sat in a winged armchair, facing the group who reclined in sofas and club chairs. Shortly after I had begun to speak, I noticed a semi-transparent ball of pale light drifting down a staircase to the left of the fireplace which passed behind the eight men facing me. I said nothing, carrying on talking until, to my amazement, the orb was followed by the semi-formed figure of a young woman. The expression on my face must have given something away, because the owner of the house asked if I was alright.

"Yes!" I replied "But were you aware that the house has a ghost?"

UNINVITED COMPANIONS

He laughed disdainfully "Surely you don't believe in spooks?"

"Well: turn and look behind you!" I responded.

The whole party swung round and looked towards the curtained windows behind them: I could tell from their reactions that they had all witnessed the young woman and had observed that her legs faded away at the knees! She gazed frankly back at us, before gradually – and there is no other word for it – dispersing like an evaporating mist.

To which of the categories listed above might this apparition have belonged? She certainly seemed aware of us, yet there was no attempt at communication and no feelings of discomfort or fear on either part.

As I drove home some hours later, I reflected on the possibility of a link between the subject of the talk (UFOs) the appearance of a bright orb and the manifestation of the young girl in Tudor costume.

Do you sometimes, out of the corner of your eyes, see a coloured glow surrounding people, plants and animals? If so, then perhaps you are one of those with an innate ability to see the aura or life-field that is held by many to be associated with every living thing in the Universe. This awareness can be developed so that it is possible, eventually, to observe the aura as readily as one might, say, observe the clothes a person is wearing, or (perhaps more exactly) the scent exuded by a flower. It is soon apparent to the adept that auras are individual in colour, texture, extent and shape: certain colours appear to be associated with the maturity of the spirit of the possessor, while sickness definitely affects the consistency and extent of this 'auric field'.

I personally find that I am only rarely aware of a person's aura unless I make a conscious effort to observe it: others I know cannot turn the ability on and off, but always see someone's aura, just as one might notice their hair colour! I do not envy this talent, which must, I would have thought, be very wearing.

UNINVITED COMPANIONS

I was aware of auras as a small child and largely took them for granted, assuming everyone could see them! The ability to observe them with greater clarity (as well as other, more singular talents) was taught to me, you will recall, by my Uncle John.

Occasionally one finds this to be a somewhat mixed blessing . . .

In the summer of 2001, my wife Linda and I were walking from a bookshop in the market region of the beautiful city of Norwich when my attention was suddenly grabbed by a blinding white sphere of light on the other side of the road. I should say that I instantly knew that whatever I was looking at had never been born upon this world! In the past I have occasionally been aware that I was in the presence of what felt like an ancient, powerful soul with an aura to match: this was not in the same category at all! What I found myself looking at was a truly malevolent entity. Perhaps more disturbingly, the creature was instantly aware of my attention: I received what I can only describe as a psychic blast of near-crippling proportions, warning me to leave well enough alone and go about my business. My mind was filled with the same aching feeling of loneliness and home-sickness that I sometimes experience when looking up into the night sky, and then the entity was gone, mingling with the weekend shoppers and soon lost among the confused background of their mental out-pourings.

I had no alternative but to stumble to a nearby restaurant for a much-needed sit-down and cup of coffee! Similar experiences have, in fact, occurred several times in the past, but never before have I felt such a malevolent mental probing: it is not impossible that the episodes of weakness and ill-health that I experienced soon after and from time to time since are connected to the strange visitor's psychic attack.

Once again, I began to consider whether there might be a connection between the different paranormal phenomena I was experiencing.

UNINVITED COMPANIONS

Some years ago I occasionally took part with hundreds of other enthusiasts in re-enactments of battles fought during the turbulent times of the English Civil War. The group to which I belonged (**The Greate Rebellion Society**) was smaller and less well-known than others, but prided itself on the accuracy of its costumes, weapons and drill and the historical research carried out by its members.

On one occasion we were due to hold a 'muster' at Cheriton, a commuter town in the South of England. Back in 1970, Cheriton was a sleepy town in Hampshire, famous only for being the site of a particularly bloody little skirmish that took place in 1643.

We were to re-enact the events that took place in what is known now (as then!) as 'The Lane of Disaster'. This sunken green-way passes between high hedgerows: back in 1643, unbeknown to a party of Parliamentarians that were marching along the lane, these hedges concealed a contingent of Royalist Dragoons. At the appropriate moment, they opened fire, wreaking havoc among the tightly-bunched foot-soldiers: hundreds were slaughtered in just a few minutes. In 1970, things were a lot more peaceful! All of us (whatever the colour of our sashes!) were camped together at one end of the lane: the village (and Inn!) were at the other!

Accordingly, after our evening meal, we formed up into a column and, colours flying and matches glowing, we marched through the dusk, down the lane to sample the local ale! When we emerged from the gloomy tunnel of the hedgerow, we found a group of two or three dozen of the villagers waiting for us: they spontaneously cheered and waved! Then, having been dismissed by our officers, we moved in groups towards the bright lights of the inn. A few of the locals walked over to us: after an exchange of pleasantries, one asked:

"So where is the other army going to be drinking?"

UNINVITED COMPANIONS

We naturally asked to which army he was referring. His reply stunned all within earshot:

"The one that marched out silently just ahead of you!"

Between them, these genuine accounts would seem to cover most of the categories of haunting described above: I could continue to add more stories of my own and those of other people I know to be truthful.

However, there are enough collections of ghost stories already available, and I have no intention of adding another! So why have I chosen these few? Firstly, because I am keen to restrict our discussion to phenomena that have occurred within the UK: that way, most of you can visit their locations, should you so wish! Secondly, of course, I decided to include, wherever possible, just my own experiences and those I have researched personally.

My own conclusions about the link between these bizarre, apparently supernatural occurrences and the topic of this book, the orb phenomenon, will become clear in the final chapters.

CHAPTER FOUR

SEARCHING FOR A PATTERN

POSSIBLY, one of the main reasons why so many people – and certainly the vast majority of scientists – dismiss out of hand accounts of supernatural goings-on like these is that there frequently seems to be absolutely no logic behind the legends. A single, repeatable paranormal occurrence in a single location might be considered if not probable, then at least possible, but that isn't how things generally happen: there appears to be a number of well-defined regions where lots of odd, apparently unrelated phenomena occur.

Consider Loch Ness: since the 'modern period' began around 1933 the Loch has reputedly been home to at least one large aquatic creature. But it is by no means the only body of water in the UK with a similar history: as well as vast basins such as Lochs Morar and Lomond, many tiny lochans in Scotland, llyns in Wales and loughs in Ireland are also said to be haunted by 'Master Otters', 'Kelpies', 'Horse Eels' and other aquatic nightmares! To me, the small size of many of these waters is very suggestive: in such tiny volumes of shallow water, could enormous living creatures *really* evade discovery or even capture for hundreds of years? Many of these lakes have been netted and dredged with not even a small bone to show for it. Surely Loch Ness (with a tradition allegedly going back to Saint Columba in the 6th Century)

UNINVITED COMPANIONS

should be full of Nessie skeletons? As we have seen, the whole region is the focus of all kinds of odd goings-on: could water monsters actually be another manifestation of this paranormal activity?

That UFOs seem to appear more often in some areas than others is certain: Cradle Hill, Warminster, Bonnybridge, Scotland, Rendlesham Forest, Suffolk, Dyfed, Wales are just a few examples. If you were really keen to see – or even photograph – a UFO, you could do a lot worse than pick one of these locations for your next holiday! As before, it is curious how frequently these places have been the sites of other paranormal happenings. The 'Welsh Triangle' for example, also has a history of bizarre humanoid apparitions, the area around Warminster is associated with big cats and crop circles, while coastal Suffolk has its own big cats, phantom dogs and green children! And, as is allegedly the case in many American UFO hotspots, 'Yeti-like' creatures have been reported in many of these places.

UNINVITED COMPANIONS

Let's throw 'ghosts' into the mix! If you think about it, there's hardly a square centimetre of the United Kingdom that hasn't witnessed violent death at some time. What with civil wars, rebellions and revolts, witch burnings, Bronze Age sacrifices and waves of invaders (including the Romans, Norsemen, Danes, Saxons, Jutes and Normans) the landscape is soaked with blood. Two World Wars during the twentieth century added tens of thousands of corpses to the pile!

Have you ever wondered why churchyards generally stand higher than their surroundings? In Norwich, for example, they are often four or five feet above the streets and footpaths that surround them. The reason is straight forward: it's the thousands of bodies that were buried and have decayed there over the millennia. Unless you bought your house directly from the builders, you can be pretty sure someone will have died there at some time, and yet we don't all live in haunted houses, and we don't have spooks turning up on all of our videos and photographs!

After a lifetime studying the supernatural, two apparently conflicting principles seem to present themselves to me:

Paranormal phenomena can occur where they seem *most* appropriate. For example, if you spent the night at the Tower of London, you might expect to see the headless apparition of Anne Boleyn.

Paranormal phenomena can occur where they seem *least* appropriate. For example, you wouldn't expect to see a Bigfoot at a UFO landing site, yet the two phenomena are not infrequently reported together in the USA.

Another thing that has always struck me is how pointless and random the behaviour of paranormal entities often seems. Why should the occupants of flying craft apparently built by highly advanced civilizations collect buckets of water from a lake, or leave complex patterns in corn fields? Why do 'spirits' at séances or TV programmes featuring celebrity mediums deliver such banal messages? ("Tell Dora the cat is here too!" is the best I've heard.)

UNINVITED COMPANIONS

Another point to ponder: unidentified aerial craft have always displayed levels of technology just a few decades ahead of the period when they were observed.

In the thirteenth century, people in Kent and Bristol supposedly witnessed sailing ships floating high above the ground: in one oft-repeated legend such a craft caught its anchor in a church steeple: a crew member climbed down to free it and, depending upon which version of the story you believe, was either stoned to death by the local villagers or else drowned in 'our world's thicker air'!

(It has to be said that the originator of the best-known story, Gervase of Tilbury, is considered a little unreliable!)

Moving forward to the late nineteenth century, we discover tales of 'Mystery Airships' in the USA and UK. Huge, apparently dirigible craft were seen travelling at high speed and with great manoeuvrability. At times just lights in the sky were observed, but occasionally witnesses were able to hold conversations with the crews: they frequently claimed to be from Mars! Reports of attempted abductions of humans and animals during the 1896 and 1897 airship waves are a curious future-echo of the UFO phenomenon.

Just after the Second World War, thousands of observers across much of Europe reported 'Ghost Rockets' crossing the sky, leaving fiery trails in their wake. After the initial reports from Finland, most of mainland Europe experienced the phenomenon: over 2000 reports were received in the peak year of 1946. Great excitement and consternation resulted, with speculation of the rockets' origin ranging from East Germany to an extraterrestrial source.

Finally, we have the situation that has obtained since the 1950s when, with human spaceflight just around the corner, people all over the world began to see advanced aircraft or spaceships that were soon universally

UNINVITED COMPANIONS

referred to as 'Flying Saucers'. Intriguingly, the occupants of these craft are often described in similar terms to some of the elementals of mythology and folklore. What's more, whether friendly to the human race ('Close Encounters of the Third Kind') or inimical ('Independence Day') these entities seem hauntingly familiar to us.

One of the arguments offered by those who do not acknowledge the reality of UFOs is their apparent extreme manoeuvrability: they have

UNINVITED COMPANIONS

frequently been witnessed carrying out stops, turns and abrupt accelerations that would kill a human being instantly. You could argue that, perhaps, their crews do not have our fragile anatomy or you might start to wonder (as I did some time ago) whether this might be evidence that they are something other than amazing pieces of engineering.

One of the strangest (and in many ways least supportable) cryptozoological themes is the idea that some of the world's remote places are the haunts of large, man-like creatures. In the Himalayas these are called **Yetis** or **Mitehs**, in North America **Bigfoot, Swamp Ape** or **Sasquatch,** and **Almas** in the Caucasus and Pamir Mountains of central Asia, and the Altai Mountains of southern Mongolia.

Despite legends and folk-beliefs going back thousands of years, there is absolutely no hard evidence for the existence of these creatures. Plaster casts and photographs of footprints, cine-film and video images, hair samples and a huge volume of eye-witness accounts: none of these constitute conclusive proof of the creatures' existence. And yet: anyone spending a week alone under canvas in the forests of Washington or British Columbia or hiking through the rhododendron thickets of Bhutan would quite possibly attach a great deal of significance to the snap of a branch nearby!

You'd think that, in a fairly heavily-populated country like the US, it wouldn't be that difficult to lay the stories of these man-beasts to rest, but still they persist. Just like UFOs, ghosts, elementals, lake monsters and orbs, logic and common sense have nothing to do with it: despite all the dismissive TV programmes, magazine articles and books, normal people continue to come into contact with them.

I'll bring this chapter to a close by reflecting on a curious truth that it has highlighted: *we humans don't even have to have personal experience of something to be affected by it!*

UNINVITED COMPANIONS

If you were to visit Loch Ness, especially if you'd never been there before, I would have a small bet that you would drive slowly along the A82 that skirts the northern shore, keeping a watchful eye out for its famous legendary inhabitant **even if you didn't really believe in its existence!**

Suppose you were to walk through Rendlesham Forest at midnight, wouldn't you feel just a little excited: apprehensive, even?

Would you spend the night locked inside a house that was said to be haunted? Or which had been the scene of a dreadful murder?

Many years ago I collected antiquarian books: I once bought a boxful at a reasonable price, among which were a few *grimoires* (books of spells!) One of these had an odd 'feel' to it (what we old hippies call a 'vibe', man!) A much more knowledgeable collector than I identified its binding as being human skin! I didn't even contemplate hanging on to it, but sold it on at the first opportunity. When I tell friends this story, they generally shiver with a little *frisson* of fear!

We all, to some extent, enjoy being frightened, especially if we are confident we are in no real danger: this is the 'appeal' that roller coasters, horror films and guided ghost tours have for many people. We can watch war films and documentaries, however harrowing, and participate vicariously in the most dreadful criminal acts, safe in the knowledge that, however terrified we may become, we can turn off the horror whenever we want to!

In the same way, newspapers and magazines have always run features purely to scare their readers. In Victorian times, these included long-running mysteries such as Spring-heeled Jack (a terrifying supernatural being that was allegedly capable of leaping over buildings) or nine day wonders like the Devil's Footprints that were found in freshly-fallen snow across much of Devon.

UNINVITED COMPANIONS

Today, such news items might include the over-stated dangers of pandemics like Swine Flu or the real or imagined threats of global warming, terrorism or asteroid impacts.

The take home message I want you to retain from this chapter is that:

Human beings are easily excited or frightened, even by the idea of things they are unlikely to experience personally!

Is there, perhaps, a single aspect of the paranormal that offers a clue to how all of these diverse and apparently unrelated phenomena might be linked? We will consider one possibility in the next chapter!

UNINVITED COMPANIONS

Apparent small elemental on Track 10, Rendlesham Forest

CHAPTER FIVE

ELEMENTAL, MY DEAR WATSON!

PLEASE don't take the trouble to write to me or to the publisher: I know Sherlock Holmes never actually said that in any of Conan Doyle's stories about the great detective! The above misquote does, however, remind us that one of the most-celebrated authors in the English language was also a firm believer in fairies, goblins and elves: elementals!

A belief that we have always shared our planet with other, non-human entities is a consistent theme in the mythologies of every culture from every period of our history.

When I was a child, someone gave me a book of poetry that, astonishingly, was considered suitable for young readers. Even sixty years later, I still recall the first verse of William Allingham's poem

'The Fairies':

Up the airy mountain,

Down the rushy glen,

We daren't go a-hunting

For fear of little men.

UNINVITED COMPANIONS

As a five year-old, I found the rest of the poem just as frightening, with its themes of abduction and enchantment. The reason I found the poem so disturbing is in its third line: if even **armed adults** are too scared to risk an encounter with the fairies, they must, I reasoned be pretty terrible creatures!

Because of this poem, I completely by-passed the 'Tansy & Bobbles' image of the Fairy Folk: I never thought of them as mischievous little sprites who sipped nectar and fluttered Tinkerbelle-like from flower to flower. Instead, I thought of them as malevolent entities that stole babies from their cribs and replaced them with changelings.

In his seminal thesis on cryptozoology **'On the Track of Unknown Animals'**, the French author Bernard Heuvelmans made a typically bold and original suggestion. He maintained that our race-memories of smaller, more primitive hominids with which we once co-existed are the basis of legends of fairies, elves, goblins, trolls and the rest of the 'wee folk'. Heuvelmans is quite rightly considered the father of cryptyozoology: his books, in my view, are the finest ever written on the subject of creatures that undoubtedly exist now or in the recent past, but which science refuses to acknowledge. In this instance, though, I can see a flaw in his argument: there are still plenty of people alive today who claim to have encountered representatives of these 'race-memories of an extinct branch of the human family tree'!

Sir Arthur Conan Doyle's most famous involvement with the paranormal is his investigation of the Cottingley Fairies. I'm sure many of you who have been kind enough to buy this book know all about this famous case: it has been much-discussed in print and on television, and was even the subject of two films. However, just in case a reminder is required, the basic facts are these: two young cousins, Elsie Wright and Frances Griffiths, took five photographs near the home of their aunt in West Yorkshire, of what appeared to be fairies and gnomes interacting with the girls. To modern eyes, in all honesty, the images seem two-dimensional and stereotypic, yet for many

UNINVITED COMPANIONS

UNINVITED COMPANIONS

years Elsie and Frances continued to claim they were genuine. Then, in 1983, the girls admitted that four of the photographs were faked. (Although both girls continued to insist that they had *seen* the little creatures!)

To me, the most fascinating aspect of the story is that Frances claimed until her death in 1986 that the fifth and final image was genuine! What are we to make of this, or the independent analyses of the picture of a goblin that concludes there is no obvious evidence of trickery? Were the girls telling the truth all along, only to succumb eventually to family pressure to say they'd faked the pictures? Or was it a harmless piece of make-believe that grew beyond the cousins' power to control?

One thing that is certain, and a point that is central to the core-thesis of this book, is that thousands of people visited Cottingley in the hope – expectation, even – of seeing fairies.

One only has to look at a gazetteer of the United Kingdom to realise how widespread a belief in 'the little people' once was: similarly, the backbone of traditional folk music is songs about Fairies and other elemental beings.

So who still sees fairies? According to author Marjorie Johnson, lots of people! Her book *'Seeing Fairies'* contains masses of data about modern encounters with a variety of types of fairy: the work makes compelling reading . . .

Through my lectures and researches, I've come to believe that the desire to experience something mysterious and out of the ordinary is very widespread. This can be an incentive for people to conduct their own investigations, join societies or attend public meetings. Or it can, undeniably, occasionally cause normally rational individuals to lose totally their powers of evaluation and discrimination. Some of this group seem to have only a very tenuous grip on reality and are often astonishingly credulous. Linda and I once attended a conference at Woodbridge where a delegate was keen to show us her

UNINVITED COMPANIONS

photographs of 'fairies' that she had taken in Rendlesham Forest the night before. Having ourselves taken similar pictures at the same time (albeit with somewhat better equipment) we gently tried to explain that her images were of Glow Worms (the phosphorescent larvae of click beetles.) She would have none of it! The pictures were shown around the room to delighted murmurs of approbation from many of the other attendees! Sometimes we see what we want to see . . .

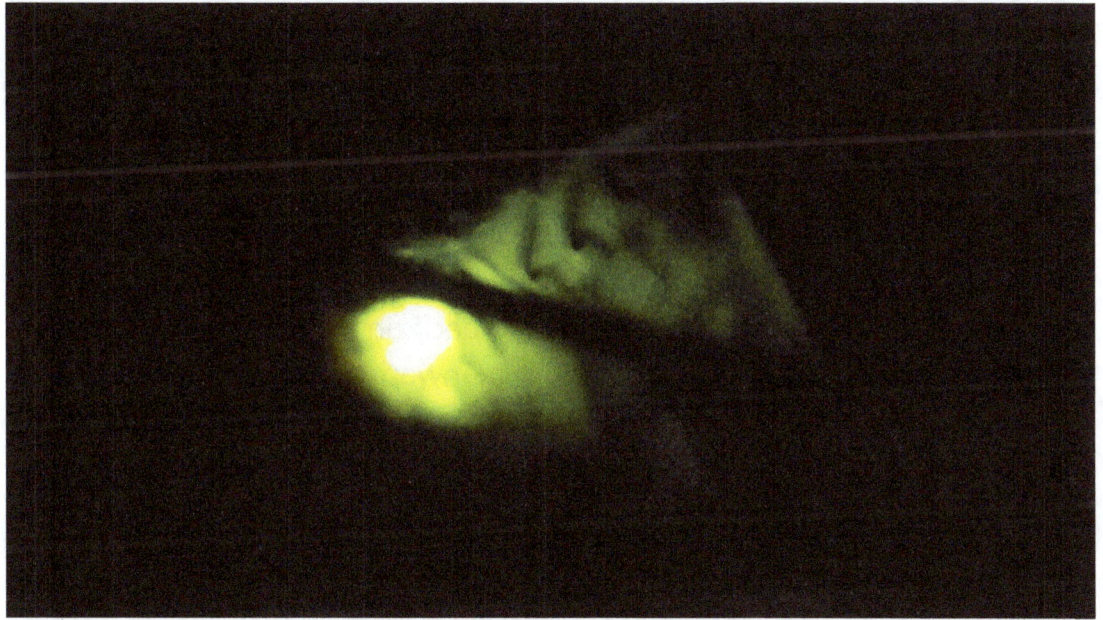

Glow worms in Rendlesham Forest

One last account in this chapter: it was told to me by an acquaintance, who often travelled away from home and family on business. This man (who we shall call John, though that isn't his real name!) is a devout Christian of a somewhat rigid disposition. He has little time for anything that smacks of the occult or arcane. (Isn't it a strange thing that so many so-called 'very religious' individuals cannot make the intellectual leap from their faith to a more general acceptance of matters spiritual and paranormal!? But I digress!)

UNINVITED COMPANIONS

Having checked into his hotel in an ancient central Scottish city, our hero ate an enjoyable meal in the restaurant before retiring to his room, intending to bathe and have an early night: his appointment the following morning was both early and very important!

Relaxed by his bath, John crawled under the heavy quilt and soon drifted off to sleep. Suddenly he was rudely awaken by the sensation of someone, or *thing,* sitting down heavily at the end of the bed. For what seemed minutes, John could not bring himself to pull the covers from his face to investigate the unexpected visitor. Abruptly, he found his mind filled with graphic and vivid images of a very sexual nature: this is not the place to be more explicit! To his somewhat puritanical soul, this was more than John could stand! He threw back the quilt and sought the cause of his interrupted sleep...

There, seated at the end of the bed, was a semi-transparent naked female, leering at him lasciviously! Falling back on his faith, John closed his eyes and began to pray. After a while, the unwanted images in his tortured mind began to fade. When John finally summoned the steel to open his eyes, so too had the strange presence.

Following a completely restless night, John checked out: needless to say, subsequent nights in Scotland were spent at a more modern hotel!

A student of the paranormal would identify this apparition as a succubus: a supernatural entity that takes female form in order to seduce men. (There is a male counterpart, known as an incubus.) Did John's strong religious convictions make him an easy target for this creature, or was it a figment of his repressed and over-dogmatic mind?

Paranormal researchers will confirm that apparently truthful reports of all kinds of elemental entities are as common now as in the Middle Ages. I myself have met hundreds of ordinary, rational people (many of whom hold down very responsible jobs) who, under sensitive questioning, have the

UNINVITED COMPANIONS

UNINVITED COMPANIONS

most amazing experiences to recount. I know teachers who swear they have seen Fairies, professional musicians who claim to have encountered Elves and Goblins and even a pilot who was adamant that he saw a Gremlin on the wing of his fighter plane during World War 2 (Exactly as portrayed in a 1950s 'B' Movie!)

Perhaps our lives have become so ordered and regulated that many of us elect to be part of a subculture that prefers to reject the accepted version of contentious historical events and find its own truths: this may be the reason why 'Conspiracy Theories' have become such a widespread feature of modern society.

Or perhaps the very fact that millions of people spend billions of hours discussing, theorising, reading and writing about the paranormal suits 'someone' just fine! We'll return to this intriguing possibility in the final chapter. Meanwhile, try to hold the accounts you've just read in your mind and reflect upon what, if anything, might provide a link between them!

CHAPTER SIX

WORMHOLES, PORTALS & INTERDIMENSIONAL HIGHWAYS!

SOMETHING that has probably occurred to many researches of the orb phenomenon is that they might, perhaps, be mechanisms which allow entities to travel back in time or to visit us from other universes. Let's examine these suggestions separately.

A popular pastime over the past few years has been searching through Internet image libraries for pictures of apparent time travellers. The social network sites have plenty of fascinating candidates, ranging from modern-looking men wearing Ray-Bans, to any number of individuals apparently talking on cell phones. There are even a few photos of modern-day celebrities apparently transported back in time: the best of these is an undoubted Nicholas Cage lookalike!

I must admit, some of these images are pretty convincing, and yet we are forced to accept the possibility that they are probably examples of the type of gratuitous coincidence that fill the books of 'Ancient Astronauts' theorists. Just because a rock painting of a figure in a tribal mask looks **to us** like an alien in a space helmet, that doesn't prove that's what is depicted!

It is a well-established principle that our eye-brain combination searches

UNINVITED COMPANIONS

for familiar patterns during image interpretation: we all saw pictures in the clouds or the Man in the Moon when we were children, and **Fortean Times** is full of simulacra: trees, rock outcrops and other natural objects that seem to resemble animals or famous people.

And yet there is a body of compelling data that suggests time travel may be possible and has occurred throughout the history of mankind: human footprints and artefacts in rock strata that predate the human era by millions of years, complex engineering in ancient devices, and legends and sacred writings that seem to refer quite specifically to technologies far in the future.

UNINVITED COMPANIONS

UNINVITED COMPANIONS

One of the greatest seekers of this kind of anomalous data was Charles Fort: he described his records as 'damned' because orthodox science chose simply to ignore them. His books are rambling collections of astonishing phenomena that he assembled during his time as a journalist and, subsequently, as a ground-breaking author. His four main works in this field – 'The Book of the Damned', 'New Lands', 'Lo' and 'Wild Talents', are filled with anachronistic occurrences: even though they are hard going, they are, in my opinion, definitely worth reading.

But there is an obvious argument against the possibility of time travel: surely, if a method of achieving it were ever going to be discovered, we'd have always known about it! Wouldn't people from the future be continually popping back to the present to avert disasters, stop the build-up of conflicts and leave us helpful items of future technology? There are several possible answers to this paradox:

- While time travel is possible, there are natural laws that prevent future generations from changing the past: if you went back in time and shot Wellington on the eve of Waterloo, one of his generals would take command and Napoleon would still be defeated.

- Time travel *is* possible but 'chrononauts' must abide by strict codes of non-intervention. There might even be 'time police' whose job it is to go back and prevent, undo or ameliorate changes.

- If a time traveller does alter the past, he merely creates another parallel universe where the change is seamlessly incorporated into history. (Suppose a Jewish time traveller went back to the 1920s and killed Hitler: he would create a world where, without a charismatic leader, the Third Reich never happened. But in *our* world, nothing was changed!)

As fascinating as it might be to consider possible natural and imposed

UNINVITED COMPANIONS

constraints on time travel, the fact is that the currently-held beliefs in physics seem to suggest that it is impossible. In the early years of the 21st century, some physicists began to speculate that hypothetical particles called tachyons might travel faster than light and, hence, move through time. This property would conflict with the Laws of Causality (events happening before their cause!) and most scientists are no longer optimistic that tachyons will ever be discovered.

However, it **has** been suggested in print (and more frequently in discussions I've had with other paranormal researchers) that orbs may be protective capsules that must be used while travelling in time. As many of you may know, one of the main witnesses to the events at RAF Woodbridge /Rendlesham Forest in December 1980 is adamant that the object which allegedly landed near the airbase was actually from the future.

Another suggestion that is often heard at UFO and paranormal conferences is that orbs contain **visitors from another dimension**.

I feel this phrase owes more to 1950s 'B-Movies' than hard science, but let's give it a few lines anyway!

What is meant by 'another dimension'? Our world is three dimensional: everything in it has length, breadth and height and the properties of surface area and volume. Because we ourselves inhabit a 3-D universe, we can easily understand realities with **fewer** dimensions, but not **more**.

A two-dimensional object has just length and breadth, with the properties of area and orientation: a one dimensional object has just length and the property of direction. (In mathematics a line is a 1-D concept: strictly speaking, a pencil line is a 2-D rectangle because the thickness of the pencil point gives it width!)

Imagine you were a 2-D character like the eponymous hero of the kids' book 'Flat Stanley'. You would have no concept of the 3-D world that I inhabit:

UNINVITED COMPANIONS

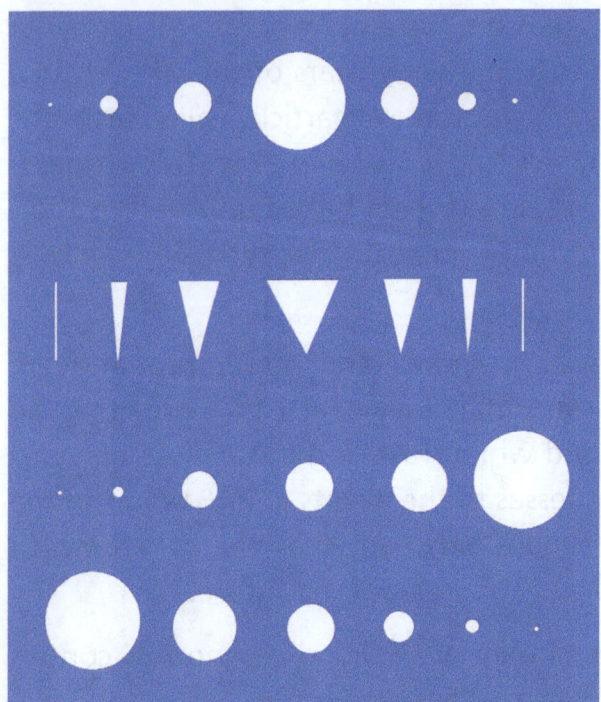

Three of these sequences represent a cone travelling through a two dimensional world. Which is the odd one out?

if I were to push a ball through your universe, you'd see a point that became an increasingly large circle before shrinking back into a point and disappearing. A cube hitting your world face-on would appear suddenly as a constant-sized square that disappeared as suddenly as it arrived! (You might like to figure out for yourself what a cone would look like to Flat Stanley, depending on whether it arrived in his world point first, base first or side-on first!)

Although some aspects of the UFO phenomenon have a faint whiff of 2-D / 3-D interaction, I reckon that when most people say 'a visitor from another dimension', they actually mean 'a visitor from a parallel universe'

A popular assumption in science fiction books and films is that, given enough energy, it should be possible to distort or 'warp' the fabric of space-time, so that two points light years apart can be brought so close together that travel between them would be virtually instantaneous.

Any reader who grew up in the sixties will be familiar with the Commander of the Starship Enterprise, Capt. James T Kirk. Several times in each episode of 'Star Trek', Kirk gives the order:

"Ahead warp factor five, Mr Sulu!"

UNINVITED COMPANIONS

Massive star warping space

This became so much a part of popular culture that many people assumed 'warp drive' was, if not a reality, then just around the corner: I ***know*** this to be true, because of comments made by audience members at my lectures

The theory behind space warping relies on the idea that time-space exists as a matrix that can actually be distorted. The deformation of this matrix by an enormous mass like a planet or star is responsible for the phenomenon we call gravity. Allegedly! It should always be borne in mind that **science does not explain things, only *describes* them!**

For example: we know by observation and experimentation that magnetism is a much stronger force than gravity (even a small magnet will pick up a needle against the pull of the Earth's gravity!) and yet no-one has

UNINVITED COMPANIONS

the slightest idea what it might be! When I was lecturing and teaching, I habitually defined a scientific 'fact' as:

'That which is currently held to be true by the majority of specialists in a given field'

Or, to put it more succinctly: there is no such thing as an absolute scientific fact, because our knowledge (or more correctly, our interpretation) of the natural world continually changes.

If you *were* able to travel back in time and attended a climate change conference in the 1970's, you'd discover that the looming problem everyone was worried about was a dramatic chilling of the Arctic Ocean and the start of another Ice Age! (Many of these theorists are, of course, the same 'experts' that now claim to have predicted catastrophic Global Warming since the 1960s!)

As recently as the 1960s, it was considered by all but a handful of astronomers and geologists that the 2000 or so large holes dotted around the world could not possibly be craters excavated by the fall of extraterrestrial masses: now the same people make dire predictions about future extinction-event sized asteroid impacts!

(I'll make a prediction of my own: as a professional meteoricist, I have been telling people for years that most of those craters were made by comets, not asteroids: I reckon that explanation will soon become the received wisdom!)

Even if there is such a thing as the 'space-time matrix' (rather than just an infinite chunk of emptiness with galaxies, dust, gas and so on dotted about in it) however much energy would it take to distort it? After all, as we have seen, even the vast mass of a star doesn't warp it *that* much!

Since we currently don't even have sufficiently energetic power plants

UNINVITED COMPANIONS

to visit even the nearest stars in the lifetime of a human being, I wouldn't put down the deposit on a trip to Vulcan just yet!

The existence of tunnels through space-time linking different points in the universe (or even different universes!) was proposed by Albert Einstein and Nathan Rosen in 1935, based on Einstein's General Theory of Relativity. It needs to be said that they only postulated tiny, unstable Einstein-Rosen Bridges, not vast tunnels that starships could travel through. And even if they existed, you'd have no control over where these bridges took you: it would be a one-way trip to who knows where!

In recent times, Einstein's model of the universe (and the various others clustered around it) has been shown to be *less* useful in describing the interaction of atom-sized systems. We actually have two apparently conflicting models: Einsteinian Relativity and the Standard Model, based upon Quantum Mechanics.

Unfortunately, gravity doesn't fit well into quantum theory: the latest attempt to integrate it into the Standard Model has produced String Theory. This is appallingly complex, but basically attempts to define particles in terms of vibrating one-dimensional 'strings': it is a desperate attempt to create a unified model of the universe! I wouldn't mind betting that only a tiny percentage of cosmologists understand string theory, but that didn't prevent the construction of the CERN Large Hadron Collider to try and find evidence that it is the definitive model of the universe.

So, when paranormal theorists suggest that orbs may be capsules to allow visiting entities to:

- **Travel in time or**
- **Travel from one dimension to another or**
- **Travel from one Universe to another through a wormhole**

UNINVITED COMPANIONS

. . . they are making a conceptual leap based on a whole bunch of unproven and barely comprehensible theories that cannot even be reconciled by the few people that claim to understand them! If we are convinced that orbs exist, there must be a simpler explanation!

CHAPTER SEVEN

PARANORMAL ENTITIES: ARE THEY *ALIVE?*

BY now, you are probably beginning to come to grips with the central theme of this book: that the many different aspects of the paranormal are in reality manifestations of a single phenomenon. But before we can reach our final consideration of the nature of the paranormal and orbs themselves, we must first reflect upon the biological meaning of the word 'alive'.

To a biologist, the word has a precise meaning, somewhat different to how it is used in general literature or conversation. Power cables are referred to as being 'live', while fires 'die'. A thunder storm may be described as 'alive with electricity': even TV and radio broadcasts are described as 'live'!

We do need an agreed definition of what actually constitutes life, so that it can be recognised even in its most exotic forms. The father of exobiology, Carl Sagan, postulated that living organisms could have evolved in even the most hostile environments: he theorised that entire ecosystems could exist in the atmospheres of gas-giant planets like Jupiter, or in oceans under the frozen surfaces of their satellites.

Years ago I was told by one of my astronomy lecturers that planets outside our solar system would never be discovered due to the vast distances

UNINVITED COMPANIONS

between our Sun and even its closest neighbours. Since then hundreds of exoplanets have been discovered and it is now axiomatic that the vast majority of stars – if not all of them – will have some form of planetary companions. Life of some form will undoubtedly have evolved on many or most them: but would we recognise it?

Our definition of life must involve all or most of the following characteristics:

- **The ability to reproduce.**
- **Some level of sentience and response to the surroundings.**
- **Growth, repair and structural change.**
- **A metabolism capable of taking energy from the environment and transforming it in order to carry out all of these.**

Non-living things may demonstrate *some* of the above: for example, a fire takes in oxygen and uses it to transform fuel in order to grow and reproduce, but it doesn't display sentience: crystals take in chemicals and energy from their surroundings and use them to grow, but don't display irritability.

Central to current definitions of life is the presence of a self-replicating molecule that can communicate genetic information from one generation to the next. So far, everything points to this 'chemistry of life' being based on the carbon atom. There's a good reason for this: having four electrons in its outermost shell, carbon is capable of forming the type of long chain molecules that are required to encode the massive amount of genetic information needed to 'construct' even a simple living cell. The molecules that perform this role in all living things on Earth are nucleic acids. In complex organisms, the genetic 'blueprint' that is used by a cell to create copies of itself or define its function is DNA (deoxyribonucleic acid) A smaller molecule, RNA

UNINVITED COMPANIONS

(ribonucleic acid) carries out the functions of DNA: transferring information needed to make proteins, for example.

In most organisms these nucleic acids are bunched into long, rod-like structures called chromosomes that are found in the nucleus of almost every living cell.

It's hard for us to conceive of a workable alternative, but, just possibly, long chain molecules based on the silicon atom might function in the same way.

OK: so bearing all this in mind, what's **the point** of life?

The world's religions all answer this question in terms of noble-sounding quests for truth, spiritual enlightenment and knowledge. Unfortunately, the empirical evidence seems to suggest that every living organism (from an Amoeba to a human being) actually exists simply in order to reproduce!

In reality, all life on our planet is really just a self-sustaining device for taking in raw materials in order to replicate itself. One of my biology lecturers liked to describe a cell as being like a car factory that carries out its function of making thousands of cars every day and then, at the end of the week, it makes another car factory too! And, of course, an entire human contains around thirty seven trillion cells!

To put this in the simplest terms, all living things carry out more or less the same basic functions. They:

- **Absorb food**
- **Break it down into small molecules**
- **Metabolise it to release energy for movement and provide raw materials for growth**

Higher plants and animals make energy by a process of aerobic respira-

UNINVITED COMPANIONS

tion: complex carbohydrates such as starches and sugars are broken down into glucose which is reacted with the oxygen we breathe in to produce water and carbon dioxide. During this process, energy is released that can be stored within cells until needed:

$$C_6H_{12}O_6 + 6\ O_2 \rightarrow 6\ CO_2 + 6\ H_2O$$

glucose   oxygen   carbon dioxide   water

(As some of you will know, aerobic respiration is a lot more complicated than this, involving the carboxylic acid cycle and the electron transport chain: this is a pretty good 'summing up', though!)

As an aside, some simple organisms can produce energy *without* oxygen: yeast, for example. Instead of water, yeast cells produce alcohol as a waste product: I sincerely thank them for their efforts!

It's an astonishing fact that most of the energy we produce this way is used just to keep our body alive and lug it around in an endless hunt for food! The brain requires about 300 calories a day, of which the actual process of thinking probably uses just 50 calories. This tiny amount of energy (about what you'd obtain from eating a small biscuit!) is involved in the membrane ion pumping that produces action potentials in the brain's neurons: these are the nerve impulses measured by EEG. (electroencephalography).

To put it succinctly, life as we know it is an incredible waste of a planet's resources! The tiny variations in the brain's energy field that are associated with the process of thinking can be detected by an EEG: this, effectively, is all we have to show for the thousands of calories of food and drink we take in every day! And, as omnivores, humans are much better at generating this energy than herbivores like cows: it is so difficult to extract energy from grass that they have to spend most of their waking lives eating.

UNINVITED COMPANIONS

Could another way of doing things have evolved, either here or elsewhere?

Can you cope with a bit more biology? I promise it'll be worth it!

Some of the most fascinating (if somewhat revolting!) organisms are parasites. These are animals and plants that don't bother to search out their own food, but steal it from other, different organisms instead. From the one-celled protozoans that live in your blood and give you malaria to the whopping great tapeworms that can inhabit your intestines, there is a huge variety of bone-idle parasites that can get a free lunch at your expense. Many of these completely lack any form of digestive system, while parasitic plants like Dodder don't have leaves. (I'm sure you know this: green plants actually make their own sugar from water and carbon dioxide, which they bind together chemically using the energy in sunlight. Dodder obtains the sugar it needs by inserting 'roots' into the food transport system of its host plants)

It does seem that the processes of natural selection and evolution eventually generate organisms that are adapted for **every** conceivable mode of nutrition: there are even moulds and bacteria that flourish in boiling hot mineral pools!

Supposing there were organisms out there – psychic parasites – that had found a way to get **their** 30 calories a day 'thinking energy' directly from the energy output of **our** brains?

UNINVITED COMPANIONS

Coalescing mist along Capel Green field margin

Structured and coloured mist, Track 10, Rendlesham Forest

CHAPTER EIGHT

ENERGY BEINGS: THE DESTINY OF INTELLIGENT LIFE?

OUR Earth is around four and a half billion years old: the Sun is a few million years older. (It's hard to be exact, since we're not entirely sure how long planetary formation takes.)

It seems pretty certain that the first, simple life appeared on Earth around three billion years ago: more complex multi-cellular organisms didn't show up until a billion years ago, while humans are real new-comers: we've only been here for a couple of million years. If the whole history of our planet were to be represented by a 24-hour clock face, humans appeared about **forty seconds before midnight!**

As we have discussed earlier, the Earth is by no means the only planet in the Universe: there are seven others orbiting our Sun as well as innumerable minor planets and satellites. Our Sun is just one of possibly four hundred billion stars in our galaxy, the Milky Way, which is just one galaxy out of at least two hundred billion in the Universe. A recent estimate put the number of planets in the Milky Way alone at one hundred billion, nearly a half of which orbit their stars in the 'sweet zone' where life would be possible. Since the Universe is thought to be around fourteen billion years old, there

UNINVITED COMPANIONS

should be plenty of planets – and civilizations – far older than ours!

There was a famous meeting of SETI (The Search for Extraterrestrial Intelligence) at Green Bank, West Virginia in 1961, during which Dr Frank Drake proposed the eponymous equation that attempted to predict the number of intelligent civilisations in the Universe which we might detect by their radio emissions:

$$N = R \times f_p \times n_e \times f_l \times f_i \times f_c \times L$$

N = the number of civilizations in our galaxy with which it might be possible to communicate

R_* = the average rate of star formation in our galaxy

f_p = the fraction of those stars that have planets

n_e = the average number of planets that could support life

f_l = the fraction of planets where life actually develops

f_i = the fraction of planets where intelligent life develops

f_c = the fraction of these that have technologies that can send detectable signs of their existence into space

L = the length of time that such civilizations remain detectable

Using the currently-held data, the number of civilizations we might detect, N, could be much higher than the one million suggested by Carl Sagan or the twelve thousand predicted by Drake.

There's a problem! As Enrico Fermi pointed out in his famous Fermi Paradox, despite looking for ET emissions since 1960, we haven't detected any signals! There are a few possible reasons for this:

- The most pessimistic (which flies in the face of all logic!) is that we haven't detected any other civilizations because they don't exist!

UNINVITED COMPANIONS

- The Drake Equation includes the factor 'L' (How long a civilization remains technologically active.) Looking back on human history, to date we've only managed a bit more than a century of radio emissions: during that time we've come perilously close to a catastrophic end to all life on Earth. Einstein was once asked what weapons would be used to fight World War Three: his reply is legendary:

'I know not with what weapons World War 3 will be fought, but World War 4 will be fought with sticks and stones.'

Another factor is that rapid global transportation allows pathogenic viruses to cross the oceans in hours. It took decades for the Black Death to reach Europe, but modern pandemics could spread to all humanity in weeks.

Then again, with or without our help, the Earth's climate is in a state of continual change. Global Warming or a new Ice Age: our modern societies wouldn't survive either in their present form.

Finally, it may be that there are much more ancient technological civilizations out there that roam the Universe eliminating the competition!

In other words, it's possible that technological civilizations are inevitably destroyed by warfare, disease, climate change or interspecific competition.

- We could be looking for the wrong signs! Just because *our* evolution has led us down the technology route, that doesn't mean *all* intelligences are fated to do the same.

- It could be that evolution inevitably produces intelligent life forms that *no longer require a solid physical body!*

As we have seen, we only use a tiny percentage of our energy intake during mental activity. And even then, a lot of this activity isn't involved in intelligent thought: some authorities claim as little as 10 calories of energy a day!

UNINVITED COMPANIONS

Suppose a life-form had evolved to the point where it could obtain this modest requirement directly from its environment. It would no longer need a physical body to hunt out and process food, a circulatory system to move it around the body, a liver to store sugar nor a respiratory system to convert it to energy! Is it inconceivable that, during the near-fourteen billion years that life has had the chance to develop and evolve out there in the Universe, myriads of intelligences have gone along this path? Since, as pure 'energy beings', they would have no further need for food, water or oxygen, they wouldn't even require a home planet: they could roam at will through the Universe. And, of course, with no body to grow old, become infected with pathogens or experience corrupt DNA replication, these entities would be immortal!

For mankind, the biggest barrier to interstellar travel is the fact that we only live seventy or eighty years: of this, we are only fit and active for fifty or so! The only way we could undertake a trip lasting a hundred years would be to be placed in suspended animation (Like Ripley in the film 'Alien'!) But even if that were possible (and no-one has yet been revived after such a procedure) what would be the point? When you returned to Earth, everyone you knew would have died a century and a half before you arrived. There'd be nobody to report to!

For our postulated Energy Beings, time would cease to be a factor in their expansion across the cosmos: being immortal, they could travel as far and as fast (or slowly!) as they wanted. And should it be proven that wormholes *do* exist, or that Black Holes are portals to other Universes, passing through either wouldn't present any difficulty to a cloud of 'thought energy'!

It might also be the case that these hypothetical entities could absorb energy directly from the space around them in the form of electromagnetic radiation or any of the other possible energetic waves or particles.

UNINVITED COMPANIONS

If this all seems a little far-fetched, just consider the fact that far more people have experienced some form of paranormal event than have travelled in space, yet most of us don't doubt the accounts of the thousand or so astronauts and cosmonauts who claim to have orbited the Earth!

Throughout history, citizens of every nation have learned to accept unquestioningly virtually all they are told by politicians, scientists, religious leaders and educationalists. Very rarely are we ever offered concrete evidence of many of the fundamental tenets of our societies, and yet we continue to meekly obey laws and regulations drawn up by people with a vested interest in our doing so! Just one non-controversial example: the current upper speed limit on Britain's roads is 70 mph. This was introduced as a two-year trial in December, 1965 in response (we were told!) to rising accident rates and was never rescinded. And yet:

- Seventeen other countries in Europe have higher speed limits with no significantly greater accident rates than that of the UK.
- There are far many more fast trunk roads and motorways now than in 1965.
- Cars have power steering, better brakes, better impact protection, better tyres, mandatory seatbelts and airbags.
- Motorways and dual carriageways have well-designed central barriers and constant monitoring of traffic flow and hazards.

If you want evidence of just how safe cars have become compared to those we drove in the 60s, consider the numbers: there are thirty five million cars registered in the UK today: in 1965, when the number was just over ten million there were nearly 400,000 serious road accidents. In 2012, this was 200,000, with a far lower fraction being fatalities.

What does this have to do with the central theme of this book? Well,

UNINVITED COMPANIONS

quite simply this: we are told from a very early age what is right, what is wrong, what we can believe in, what we can't: what to think, what to say and what to accept at face value. We have become institutionalised in a total fulfilment of Huxley, Bradbury and Orwell's dystopian views of the future! We have become blinkered and unquestioning: as long as there's something decent on the 'box', a bottle on the table, or, if that's your thing, a 'spliff' in the ashtray, we're content!

I taught across all the phases in schools during my career, until, after 35 years, I left in dismay at how the aim of the profession had seemingly mutated from *education* to *indoctrination*. The widely-used QCA schemes appeared to be crammed full of politically-inspired half truths, undistributed premises and unscientific propaganda. It seemed to me that students were discouraged from developing the ability to make the conceptual leaps that characterise innovation and discovery or from questioning the textbook 'facts', exam regurgitation of which would get them their A/S level in Science. I doubt that Newton, Wegener, Einstein and other great, original thinkers would achieve high grades in modern schools!

The majority of attendees at my lectures about paranormal, supernatural and cryptozoological themes tend to be in their late middle age: usually, there are hardly any young people in the audience. This, I feel, can only be because they have been fed a diet of dismissive incredulity by the media and education system: I was once talking to a group of sixth formers about meteorites and passed around a Campo del Cielo iron sample. I suppose I got a little 'gushy': I generally do! After all, this silvery chunk was over four billion years old, was probably once part of the core of a planet and had arrived on Earth from outer space as a screeching fireball! The first person to hold it was a sixteen-year old boy, who frowned at it for a second or two, before asking:

"Can you eat it? Can you smoke it? Can you put your hand up its jumper?

UNINVITED COMPANIONS

No! So what's it good for? Nothing!"

(I've since found that even this wasn't an original thought, but at the time it did at least make me smile!)

So, as we reach the concluding section of the book, I ask – whatever your age or background – that you suspend your disbelief for a while and consider the possibilities I put before you!

UNINVITED COMPANIONS

'Wormhole'?

CHAPTER NINE

TOWARDS AN UNDERSTANDING

So far we have examined many of the paranormal phenomena which defy logical explanation, but which, even in our pragmatic society, continue to intrigue and challenge us. Time for a few more anecdotes, which hopefully will support the conclusions we're heading towards!

Twenty years ago I was a lot more sociable than I am today: my wife Linda and I frequently hosted dinner parties at our house in Norfolk's Broadland and, although I say it myself, I had a bit of a reputation as a cook!

On this particular occasion eight people sat down to dine, and were quickly at ease in each other's company. The food and wine were sumptuous and the evening promised to be memorable . . . but not in the way that transpired! For totally unexpectedly, this urbane soiree was to provide four of the diners with their first contact with another reality.

The Thai Crab patties had just been consumed with relish and cleared away, and pan-roasted sea bass brought to the table, when a female guest (at the time, my Teaching Assistant) became aware of a presence building up in the kitchen over my shoulder. (You should know that the dining room and kitchen of the house are separated only by a chest-high brick divider and are linked by a one metre wide corridor to the rest of the house)

UNINVITED COMPANIONS

She decided to say nothing, feeling that to do so might shatter the ambience of the meal! In the event, one of the other guests sat up in his chair, his face suddenly pale.

"I just saw . . . someone . . . something . . . walk down the corridor!" he blurted. "Just an outline . . . kind of . . . grey and hazy. But there was definitely something there!" This guest and his wife (who was sitting opposite her husband) both happen to be pragmatists and – perhaps worse! – Clinical Psychologists! The wife regarded her husband sceptically with a **very** raised red eyebrow.

At this point I leaned forward and confided that I too had seen the spectral figure . . . had in fact been watching her (for it was an elderly woman who had visited the gathering) for some time!

Another female guest quickly added her supporting observations. "Nonsense!" rejoined the female psychologist. "It has been shown that the retinas of people over the age of forty undergo changes that produce just these kinds of 'flashback' images! Isn't that so, darling?" (This to her husband!) His composure having been somewhat restored by liberal draughts of good red wine, he gratefully agreed with his wife!

This 'explanation' somewhat avoids the issue of how seven people (one of whom was considerably younger than forty!) could independently witness a similar manifestation! Still, some people will **always** resist the urge to believe even the evidence of their scientifically trained eyes!

I know for an absolute fact that no-one has died in our house: furthermore, it was built on open farmland, so an old lady in 1950s clothing had no real excuse for invading the dinner party! The female guest who had first witnessed the apparition confided to me later that she had recognised the old woman as being her grandmother. Now why on Earth should this person wish to materialise so publicly, somewhere she had never visited and

UNINVITED COMPANIONS

in front of seven people she had never met? What's more, there seemed to be no purpose to her visit: she said nothing and did very little!

Strange to say, although this was the first time my Teaching Assistant had encountered the apparent ghost of her grandmother, it was by no means the last: the old woman subsequently popped in to her house for several visits, until her granddaughter moved away.

What are we to make of this? The only rationale I can offer is that the apparition, whatever its true nature, had taken on a plausible form, ***intended to create the greatest possible outpourings of psychic energy.***

Many years ago, I owned a small hotel on the cliffs above the sandy beach that separate the small town of Gorleston from the North Sea. During the summer this small establishment was crowded with families from the Midlands and North of England. During the winter, though, things were very different: the drudgery of cooking and serving over a hundred meals a day was replaced by a more relaxed, companionable atmosphere, as engineers working in the nearby gas-rig yards occupied the thirty or so rooms we kept open out of season. The hotel income was topped up by regular parties of sea anglers, for in those days the North Sea still held good stocks of cod and whiting that could be caught from the short pier south of the harbour-mouth.

One bitter December evening, a particularly amiable pair of Londoners called Mick and Roger invited me to join them on the pier to try our luck. I supplied the bait, lit the Tilley lamps and made flasks of steaming tea laced with whiskey. By 8.00pm we were by our favourite South-facing set of railings, enjoying the usual friendly banter and concentrating on the steady dipping of our rod-tips. A couple of hours passed.

Suddenly our idyll was broken by an urgent call for help from further along the pier:

UNINVITED COMPANIONS

"Give me a hand lads! I'm into a good'n here!"

The cry had come from an elderly man who lived a few doors down from the hotel: his rod was hooped over and the taut line sang in the winter wind. Roger and I ran over, leaving Mick to watch our six rods. It was immediately obvious that the old gentleman was trying to winch in a very heavy weight against the pull of the tide: his old-fashioned wooden centre-pin reel was making the job extremely difficult for him. Roger suggested that he and I try to hand-line the 'fish' to the base of the pier, where we could scoop it up in a large drop-net: to this the old man readily agreed.

Fitting the deed to the word, Roger and I pulled together on the thick line until the object at its end cleared the water ten feet below us. Mick had by now joined us with the net. He shone a powerful torch downwards: all four of us were appalled to see the unmistakeable form of a long-dead corpse: to add to the horror of the moment, a number of sleek, fat eels slithered out from between the ribs and fell into the sea with an audible 'plop'.

Fortunately there was, at the time, a Coastguard lookout at the end of the pier: Roger ran for help while (trying not to look too closely!) I tied off the line to a stanchion.

For the next hour we recounted our tale: first to the Coastguard, then to the Police. The corpse was retrieved and taken away, and my two friends and I decided that enough was enough: we headed back to the cliff steps and home, with our somewhat shaken elderly companion tagging along.

As we reached the top of the steps, we turned back for a final look at the sea. Where before it had seemed familiar, with the promise of sport to come, it now looked dark and forbidding. Suddenly a movement at the water's edge caught our attention: loping across the pale sand and seemingly glowing in the winter moonlight was the form of a huge black dog with eyes that,

UNINVITED COMPANIONS

even at a distance, glowed fire-red! The old man gave a low moan:

"That's Shuck, that is . . . The Hell-Dog that turns up when there's death about!"

Whether it was the traumas of the evening, or natural causes, the elderly fisherman never left his bed again: he went down with a chesty cold and died a fortnight later.

As with all the other experiences in this book, this is a genuine account of that night's events. What makes it so bizarre (and of significance to the present work) is the fact that it involves two kinds of unsettling event: one real and one paranormal and, perhaps, ultimately fatal.

Something that may have occurred to you straight away is that the old man had **absolutely no**

A straunge and terrible Wunder wrought very late in the parish Church of Bongay, a Towun of no great distance from the citie of Norwich, namely the fourth of this August, in ye yeare of our Lord 1577. In a great tempest of violent raine, lightning, and thunder, the like whereof hath been sel= come seene.
With the appearance of an horrible sha= ped thing, sensibly perceived of the people then and there assembled.
Drawen into a plain method ac= cording to the written coppe.
by Abraham Fleming.

UNINVITED COMPANIONS

evidence that what he was looking at was not just a large feral dog with unusual eyes: his immediate assumption was that he had witnessed the legendary Black Shuck. Having seen for myself how frightened he was by the event, I can confirm that this was one of those times when a strongly-held conviction can affect someone as traumatically as a physical assault.

There is a widespread belief that numbers of alien wild animals roam the British countryside: hardly a week passes without a newspaper account of an anomalous big cat popping up somewhere. Considering how densely populated and increasingly urbanised the UK has become, logic dictates that these pumas, lions, panthers and lynxes cannot exist: yet people continue to see them and even shoot them! In 1991 a European Lynx was shot dead by a gamekeeper near Great Witchingham, Norfolk. The default response by the Police and media was that the animal had escaped from a wildlife park (it hadn't!) or was an illegally-released pet. But who would spend a small fortune on an exotic pet only to turn it loose into the countryside? In East Anglia, US servicemen who are about to return to their home country are often held accountable: to me this seems most unlikely and a little stereotypic!

Generally speaking reports of ABCs (alien big cats) and other out-of-place wildlife trigger a desultory police investigation and a brief reference as the last item on the 10 o' clock news! The true situation, in my estimation, justifies a far more rigorous approach. Since my **Chilling Tales UK** website went online in 1999, I have researched several dozen accounts of anomalous creatures from a complete cross-section of the British population. Ordinary people in areas where ABCs suddenly appear often have their lives disrupted for weeks, months or even years. After all: would you cheerfully allow your children to go and play in fields of long grass where a lioness had been seen a few weeks previously?

UNINVITED COMPANIONS

The following encounter was reported by Malc, an Australian teacher who was starting a two-year contract in the UK at a school I frequently visited. One day he stopped me in the staffroom to ask:

"Hey listen, mate! You know about animals: do you get Panthers in the UK?"

My reply was non-committal, but I enquired why he asked such an apparently bizarre question! He responded with the following account:

The previous weekend, he had been driving along the A47 towards Kings Lynn from Norwich. As he neared the familiar twin wind turbines at Swaffham, he was forced to brake abruptly to avoid running into the rear of the car in front: this had swerved and slowed unexpectedly for no obvious reason. To Malc's astonishment, an enormous black cat crossed the road in front of the stationary vehicles, before loping up the embankment and disappearing. Malc, his wife and two children witnessed the whole amazing occurrence from a range of around thirty yards! His description was the classic: a heavily-built black cat with a long, drooping, muscular tail, somewhat larger than an Alsatian dog.

The Australian teacher was genuinely surprised by the interest his account generated among the rest of the staff: he really had no idea that large black cats aren't a feature of the British countryside!

This, and a large volume of similar reports by reliable witnesses, have led me to the belief that many, if not all, of these creatures are in the same category as the lake monsters we considered earlier. Although apparently flesh and blood, the sheer impossibility of their continued unconfirmed existence suggests that they may be part of the phenomenon that is the topic of this book.

I must now turn to a somewhat controversial topic: religion, its visions

UNINVITED COMPANIONS

and holy places. Are there connections between orbs and their associated phenomena and Man's long-standing belief in a supernatural creator?

CHAPTER TEN

"IF GOD DID NOT EXIST, WE WOULD HAVE TO INVENT HIM."

AS I'm sure you know, this is the French writer Voltaire's assessment of the importance of religion to humanity.

Have you attended or witnessed television broadcasts of a Papal Mass, or the procession of pilgrims around the Kaaba in Mecca during Hajj? The expressions on the faces of Sikhs visiting the Golden Temple at Amritsar or Jews praying at the Wailing Wall in Jerusalem leave us in no doubt about the intensity of the worshippers' emotions. As one who doesn't subscribe to any organised religion, I find these spectacles difficult to understand but totally astonishing.

Since the dawn of civilization, when the discovery of stock-herding and agriculture freed our ancestors from the need to spend their waking hours hunting and gathering food, our ancestors started to look for answers to these timeless questions:

- Where did we come from?
- What happens to us when we die?
- Are we special or are we just clever animals?
- Does mankind have a pre-ordained destiny?

UNINVITED COMPANIONS

From the most ancient times, mankind's attempts to answer these questions generated the idea that we have some kind of immortal soul that enters our bodies during conception and leaves at the point of death. Where it goes after that is what defines – and divides – many of the world's great faiths.

From cave paintings in France and Australia, to temples and pyramids in Egypt and South America, to great cathedrals, mosques and mandirs, our world shows ample evidence of the impact of religion in our lives – whether we like it or not! Try buying a loaf of bread after 4.00pm on a Sunday in a British supermarket!

To anyone who studies religion from the 'outside', the most astonishing manifestations of fervour and faith are those displayed by believers at the world's holy places. This is particularly noticeable at Catholic Marian Shrines such as Lourdes, Fatima and Knock. At each of these locations, one or more ordinary people ranging in age from 3 to 74 witnessed alleged apparitions of the Virgin Mary. All three have become places of pilgrimage, with many claimed miraculous healings, particularly at Lourdes.

Fatima stands aside from the other two, in that in 1917, the Virgin Mary reportedly told three great secrets to the three Portugese children, Lucia dos Santos, Jacinta Marto, and Francisco Marto who reported the original apparition. These secrets have gradually been released by the Catholic Church: the first is a vision of Hell, the second refers to the twentieth century's two World Wars and the third (which may or may not have been published in full) concerns, among other things, coming dangers to the Holy See and the Catholic Church.

Of great significance to this book are the events of October 13th 1917, when a huge crowd estimated to number as many as 100,000 people witnessed a 'solar miracle' just after midday. Although accounts vary, the most frequently reported phenomenon was a change in colour and radiance

UNINVITED COMPANIONS

of the Sun, following which it appeared to spin and move around the sky. Puddles of recently-fallen rainwater allegedly dried up in minutes.

The size of the crowd in this photograph is astonishing: on the say-so of three very young children, thousands of people stood patiently in a field for hours before apparently witnessing what seems to modern minds like a UFO close encounter of the first kind! Just imagine the outpourings of psychic energy that must have occurred on **this** occasion.

Of more significance, something approaching this level of expectation and fervour still occurs on a regular basis at Fatima and a number of other shrines, **without anything else supernatural taking place!**

UNINVITED COMPANIONS

This, to a lesser extent, is the case in **any** church in **any** country during **any** service! Weddings, funerals, christenings, bar and bat mitzvahs and all the many other ceremonies that take place will generate at least some emotional or psychic energy. And remember: all of this religious tradition was inspired by a handful of simple prophets over a short period of time thousands of years ago!

A dichotomy that presents itself to all students of religion is summed up in this 1906 quote by US writer Abraham Miller:

"Many deeds are enacted in God's name which fill the Devil's heart with envy."

This quote is a reference to the countless atrocities that have been carried out throughout the centuries, using sacred scriptures as a *rationale*. The persecution of European Jews, the excesses of the Spanish Inquisition, the rape of Central and South America by the Conquistadores, the virtual genocide of native people's throughout Africa, Polynesia and North America and the atrocities committed by both sides during the current and ongoing confrontation with fundamentalist Islamic groups all find their justification in religious doctrine.

As a child, I was confused by a belt buckle that a relative had given me: its design included a swastika, which I recognised as the symbol of the evil Nazi Party, and yet it bore the motif 'Gott mit uns' which I was told meant 'God with us' How could this be true?

UNINVITED COMPANIONS

Later I discovered that every army (apart from Communist ones!) went into battle under some kind of religious mandate: from Crusaders and Saracens to Royalists and Roundheads, every soldier is told he is fighting for a just and righteous cause and, for this reason, God will protect him in battle.

Later still, I reached the conclusion that most wars – if not all – start as a result of ideological or economic competition. The only winners on either side are the arms manufacturers and victorious generals and very few foot-soldiers even understand the cause for which they are fighting.

But again: consider the phenomenal outpourings of pain, fear, anguish, elation and exultation before, during and after a battle. Although Gavrilo Princeps fired the shot that effectively started World War 1, what inspired him to do so? Are wars yet another source of thought energy for our theoretical psychic parasites? Is that why they continue to break out for no obvious gain to the majority?

Unlike me, my wife Linda is not a massive fan of History as an academic discipline. Although we have light-hearted arguments about this, she frequently makes an inarguable point: if we ever learned anything by studying History, there would only ever have been one war! And you'd think that politicians would consider the total collapse of British industry, economy and global influence following World War 2 before involving the country in further conflicts. Yet since 1945 the British Army has enjoyed only one year without being involved in fighting somewhere:

Korea, Suez, Aden, Cyprus, Malaya, Kenya, Falklands, Ireland, Iraq (twice!), Afghanistan and Libya is the list up until 2015.

UNINVITED COMPANIONS

Track 10 in Rendlesham Forest: scene of many strange occurrences!

CHAPTER ELEVEN

CAN PARASCIENCE EVER BECOME SCIENCE?

AT the start of this book I hinted that what I was trying to achieve was a 'Unified Theory of the Paranormal'. Human beings have experienced and recorded strange, inexplicable events since civilization began, but by their nature, they totally defy any attempt at scientific investigation. Because these phenomena are unpredictable and unrepeatable, they have generally been dismissed as misinterpretations of the mundane, exaggerated claims by witnesses or downright hoaxes.

That the paranormal undoubtedly *does* attract its share of eccentric or over-credulous disciples is undeniable. The uncritical acceptance of uncollaborated testimony, lack of rigour in record keeping, and, often, a lack of a broad general knowledge that would help eliminate spurious data, all contribute to the dismissive attitude of conventional scientists.

When astronomer Ian Ridpath dismisses the Rendlesham Forest UFO encounter as being caused by an unusual combination of several events (including meteors, a re-entering Soviet satellite and a lighthouse observed through gaps in the trees) the general public breathes a metaphorical sigh of relief and doesn't bother to check whether any of these were factors on December 30th, 1980. This is, of course, extremely frustrating for the many dedicated researchers who believe they have eliminated Ridpath's

UNINVITED COMPANIONS

suggestions by careful on-the-spot investigation and witness interviews, but in reality, the astronomer is merely applying the conventional scientific approach to such problems. No doubt, in his view, it's not up to him to disprove the reality of the Rendlesham Forest Incident, it's up to those who believe it occurred to establish that **beyond doubt**.

The same sceptical approach is brought to bear on every aspect of the paranormal. But this isn't some covertly orchestrated program of disinformation, it's just how science works! The Scientific Method, (in a simplified form) follows this kind of procedure:

- During his work, a researcher observes something new or unexpected.
- He carefully records the exact variables and physical conditions (reagents, temperatures, voltages, timings and so on).
- He attempts to reproduce the original conditions and looks for a similar outcome. This he will repeat a number of times, collecting sufficient data to eliminate the possibility of random variation.
- Once he is certain he has identified something novel, he will write a paper about his work giving full details of his procedures and a complete set of carefully checked results. This will be submitted to experts in the field for **peer review**.
- If his fellow scientists confirm the rigour of his methods, the accuracy of his calculations and the credibility of his conclusions, he will publish his work as a 'paper' in some learned journal.
- Over the following years, other researchers will attempt to emulate the original procedures and look for applications.
- If the researcher's original discovery is found to be repeatable, his
- Conclusions will become accepted as a fact by the scientific community.

UNINVITED COMPANIONS

All this is exactly what Sir Peter Scott and Robert Rines **did not** do when they announced that they had conclusive proof of the existence of the Loch Ness Monster! They held a press conference at which Rines showed heavily computer-enhanced versions of his underwater images, and announced the discovery of a new species. Somewhat prematurely, Sir Peter had even given the proposed species a name: *Nessiteras rhombopteryx*. Unsurprisingly, their claims were met with universal derision by the scientific community, not the least when this proved to be an anagram of **'Monster hoax by Sir Peter S'**!

As we move inexorably towards the concluding chapter of this book, we begin to realise why a general acceptance of its themes by 'the scientific establishment' is never likely to happen. None of the paranormal phenomena I have examined in this book is capable of any kind of true scientific investigation: UFOs just seem to turn up somewhere, carry out random operations and depart. Sometimes they appear on radar, more often they don't. Ghosts seem reluctant to perform for video cameras and leave only the most difficult to interpret messages on researchers' sound recorders. Crop circles, however complex and quickly they may form, are easily dismissed as the work of 'agricultural students' or drunks with a ball of string and a couple of planks. Lake and Sea Monsters, Abominable Snowmen, Thunderbirds, Mothmen and the other cryptozoological species just don't leave hair, bones, blood or any tangible – or testable – material in their wake. And, of course, if film special effects experts can produce CGI as convincing as that in Independence Day or Jurassic Park, why is it that all photos of paranormal subjects are blurred and dim? (Unless they're *not*, in which case they are always labelled as fakes! Catch-22!)

The key word is 'repeatable': unless something can be observed or created at will, it will never be accepted by mainstream science. Although . . . There are, in fact, quite a lot of creatures, objects and phenomena which enjoy complete acceptance by the scientific community as the real deal, despite

UNINVITED COMPANIONS

having only been observed once or twice. The existence of an example we mentioned earlier, ball lightning, is never questioned. Somewhat curiously, this elusive and largely unrepeatable plasma is even used to explain some UFO accounts!

Our understanding of the early stages of the evolution of birds from small theropod dinosaurs is largely based upon a few fossil specimens, the best known of which are the literal handful of Archaeopteryx remains. There are so many significant differences between these that many palaeontologists argue that the twelve so far recovered may well represent different species!

The fossil record of human evolution is even sketchier, often consisting of just one or two very incomplete 'type' specimens of many of the intermediate stages. Often only a couple of teeth, a leg bone or a fragment of skull are all that have been discovered to fill gaps of several hundred thousand years. Supposing a visitor on a collecting trip from another world arrived in the Congo and abducted an Ituri Pygmy. Or suppose he landed in New York and captured a member of a basketball team. Would it be reasonable for him to base his assessment of the human race on either of these single specimens?

Bizarrely, there are better photos of some disputed creatures than of some that are totally accepted by science: several pictures of the supposedly-extinct Thylacine and the Queensland Marsupial Tiger have been obtained using automatically triggered trail cameras, for example.

It is the apparent dichotomy between what is accepted by science and what is not that has altered public perception: where once chemists, physicists and doctors were treated as celebrities, now they are viewed with distrust by some, indifference by others. Yet, strangely, the modern approach to government (the "problem-reaction-solution" paradigm) has invested immense power in Scientists. Just consider some 'problems' identified in recent decades:

UNINVITED COMPANIONS

- Swine flu. Allegedly this pandemic killed half a million people before the virus burned itself out in 2010: not before literally billions of doses of vaccine were administered worldwide, however! This figure has been questioned by researchers around the globe and certainly is a huge overstatement. It has been demonstrated that the immensely costly vaccination programme in the US **possibly** saved 300 lives: that is the number of Americans murdered in just one week!

- The hole in the Ozone Layer. The Ozone Layer is actually a region of the upper atmosphere where ultra-violet radiation converts normal molecules of oxygen (made up of two atoms) into unstable triatomic ozone:

$$O_2 \text{ in the presence of ultraviolet} \rightleftharpoons 2O$$

Again, using the energy from incoming UV radiation, one of these *atoms* of oxygen then reacts with a *molecule* of oxygen to form Ozone:

$$O + O_2 \rightleftharpoons O_3$$

The point to note is that this process is reversible: the newly-formed ozone molecules are unstable and spontaneously degrade back into diatomic oxygen. Their formation absorbs a lot of potentially harmful radiation, however. So all the hype about CFCs (propellant gases in aerosols and coolants in refrigerators) destroying the ozone layer so that we'd all die of skin cancer was a little overstated: it's the formation of ozone that protects us, not the ozone itself. In May 2015, it was reported that satellite observation revealed that the holes in the ozone layer over both poles had more or less healed up again (That must've been a relief for the penguins: they could return to using spray-on underarm deodorant!)

- Creutzfeldt–Jakob disease (CJD) When this 100% fatal disease was first identified in the UK, a rapid connection was made with Bovine

UNINVITED COMPANIONS

Spongiform Encephalopathy (BSE) In the ensuing panic, five million British cattle were slaughtered, devastating the meat, dairy and tallow industries. Politicians appeared on TV eating beefburgers with their children to prove how safe British meat was, but confidence in the UK's agricultural output suffered an irretrievable setback. In 2014 the number of deaths from CJD in the UK was just over 100, compared to 10,000 plus from 'flu.

- Asteroid impact. Fifty years anyone who seriously suggested that life on our planet could be wiped out by a chunk of space-debris would have been considered slightly loopy! In 1968, I remember suggesting in a mock 'S' Level answer that the extinction of the dinosaurs might have been precipitated by such an impact. I received no marks for that question and was told by the Head of Science not to be 'a dilettante'! Now we are bombarded with gloomy predictions about forthcoming impact events by groups like the B612 Foundation: there has even been a spate of films on the theme. The threat can only be addressed, of course, by increased funding for NASA and other organisations who track rogue asteroids and plot ways of bringing about their destruction.

These are just a few of the less-contentious examples of the extent to which science has become a political tool. I consider myself as a scientist by profession and avocation and know quite a few more. (My brother is one of the UK's leading pharmaceutical and agricultural chemists) After a bottle or two of claret, most of them become quite vocal about the constraints they face: these are generally along the line

'Support the official version or lose your funding.'

Is it likely, then, that professional scientists are going to be prepared to raise their heads above the parapet and express a contrary opinion? You

UNINVITED COMPANIONS

have only to reflect upon the way 'Global Warming Deniers' like Nigel Calder and David Bellamy were treated to know the answer!

In the past, I frequently lectured about meteoritics at venues around the UK: on three occasions I participated in the BBC's 'Stargazing Live' productions. I am occasionally asked at these lectures whether I '...believe all that flying saucer rubbish!' I was brought up to always tell the truth as I see it, so (having personally witnessed several UFOs) to the surprise of my audiences, I have always responded that I do. The usual result is that I'm not invited back!

Given the current reinvention of science as a justification for some of the worst excesses of political chicanery, (WoMD anybody?) is it likely that we will see university faculties **openly** dedicated to the investigation of ghosts, UFOs and elemental spirits?

There was a brief period during the 1960s and 1970s when a belief in all things metaphysical and supernatural was far more prevalent than it seems to be today. Through books, films and music, the Hippy movement spread outwards from the west coast of the United States until the youth of most continents had been touched by it in some way. The use of psychoactive and hallucinogenic drugs became widespread and under their influence (and disenchanted with the consumerist lifestyle and political aggression of their parents) many young people anticipated an Aquarian Age of peace love and harmony. Far out, Man!

It didn't take long for this utopian vision to be crushed, subverted or subsumed: by the 1980s almost all that was left was the music and the drugs.

UNINVITED COMPANIONS

Green orb

CHAPTER TWELVE

UNINVITED COMPANIONS

'M sorry you've had to wade through eleven chapters to reach the central thesis of this book, but, well done for sticking at it: here we are!

When I started teaching and lecturing over forty years ago, I was given a piece of advice that I generally kept in mind throughout my career:

Don't start a lesson with a recap of the previous one!

Good advice, too! Nevertheless, that's what I intend to do now, mainly because the path along which we have travelled to arrive here has been so convoluted.

In the preceding pages, I've presented you, the reader, with a number of anecdotes concerning the paranormal: let me say straight away that they are, as far as I can ascertain, absolutely true. (By which I mean that I have no reason to doubt the word of the people who told me the stories: perhaps just as well, since many of the accounts are mine!)

I have suggested above that many paranormal phenomena display certain common characteristics. I believe that an examination of this connecting thread will ultimately provide evidence of an underlying cause of them all.

UNINVITED COMPANIONS

I'll list these apparent links in bullet-list form for ease of reference, before considering in greater detail what they might tell us:

- On occasion, **all** of the various phenomena we have considered above demonstrate **sentience** (awareness of what's going on around them) and **irritability** (a response to these stimuli.) For this reason I am going to assume from now on that the majority are some form of intelligent, living entity.

- Paranormal phenomena often generate fear or high levels of excitement in witnesses: this endures well after the causative event has finished and can be communicated to others, **even if they weren't personally involved.**

- They are generally unpredictable and do not occur 'to order'. Every angler is aware of the **certainty** that, following hours of inactivity, pouring out a cup of tea will produce an instant bite indication. This also appears to be the case with the paranormal: things happen when you least expect them.

- To the frustration of researchers, many paranormal events seem to have an adverse effect on cameras and electrical equipment: this happens too frequently to be just a coincidence. During the many years and thousands of hours crews from the Loch Ness Investigation Bureau spent manning cameras overlooking the Loch, they only managed one slightly disappointing piece of footage. This was not because the volunteers didn't see the monster, but rather that when it *did* appear, camera batteries would be found to have suddenly gone flat, crews were changing over or some other distraction prevented good images. Even the one piece of film that was obtained was of an object swimming past in mid-loch, as distant as it could possibly be from the paired camera rigs on either shore!

UNINVITED COMPANIONS

- An obvious point: people generally experience things where, when and how they might be *most* likely to occur. (There's no reason why you shouldn't see a UFO over the Tower of London, but most odd encounters there seem to involve headless ghosts!) Except: at times things also occur in the *least* likely places (Giant water monsters in tiny land-locked Irish loughs, for example.) If you allow my assumption that paranormal phenomena are generated by intelligent entities, this suggests two behavioural strategies are involved.

  The first takes advantage of the human propensity for 'alert expectation': this is defined by psychologists as a state of heightened awareness in anticipation of an event. This can be as mundane as the escalating excitement of a crowd before the start of a football match or as stomach-churning as the dread some people feel when a police officer approaches their car with a breathalyser in his hand! It is also the cause of the sense of anticipation felt by thousands of tourists who drive past Loch Ness every summer.

  The second capitalises on our adrenaline response to fear or excitement: when someone plays a practical joke by jumping out of a cupboard, the victim experiences a spectrum of emotion: an initial surge of fright and surprise, followed by relief (that it was just a friend playing a trick) and, often, anger at being made to look stupid or feel scared.

- As we investigate the paranormal, we seem to come across evidence of elite groups of humans with specific arcane knowledge in every area: in the past these would have been witches and wizards, and senior members of organised religion and monarchies. Today, these seem largely to have been supplanted by leaders of the industrial-military complex, intelligence agencies and a handful of carefully

UNINVITED COMPANIONS

selected individuals from financial and political backgrounds. The flow of information about the paranormal is rigorously controlled by these groups, presumably for their own ends, and possibly by other shadowy cabals such as MJ-12, the Bilderberg Group and Bohemian Grove.

Is there a single explanation for all of the paranormal phenomena experienced by human civilisation, now and throughout history? And for all the points made above? I believe there is.

Whoever's view of human evolution you subscribe to (and the biology, despite what is generally believed and taught in schools, is by no means cut and dried!) there is reasonable consensus between archaeologists, palaeontologists and evolutionists about the dates and locations of human civilisation.

I might mention that here is some compelling evidence that *other* technological races occupied the Earth long before we did, but putting that aside for the moment, it seems certain that our *current* civilisation stretches back to beginnings in half a dozen disparate centres, from the Middle East, to the Far East, to South America. This, in itself, is strange: did this quantum leap in the organisation of human society *really* occur spontaneously in places so far apart?

The usual definition of civilisation is based around the abandonment of a nomadic hunter-gatherer way of life, replacing this with the establishment of permanent settlements dependent on agriculture, a water supply and the emergence of a ruling elite: someone had to make laws to live by and ensure that they were followed!

It is generally agreed that this change first took place in the Middle East in the 10th Century BC (or BCE, if you insist!), with other civilised societies springing up in China (8th Century BCE) and Mesoamerica and Peru a few

UNINVITED COMPANIONS

hundred years later. To buy into this as a series of linked events, you'd have to assume that humans (taking their herds, crops and new-found skills) moved eastwards from Mesopotamia to the Yangtse region, north to the Bering Strait land bridge, across to North America and then south, leaving no records of permanent settlement until they reached Mexico! Here they discovered how to cultivate maize, potatoes, tomatoes and many other excellent crops. (Which begs the question: what did they eat on the journey south?)

The locations of the first half-dozen 'proper' cities are contentious, depending on which definition of a city you use: but they are probably to be found among this list:

- Uruk, in Mesopotamia, first settled around 4500 BCE
- Eridu, nearby, was thought of as the first city in the world by the Sumerians
- Byblos, a Mediterranean City in the Lebanon
- Jericho, on the west bank of the Jordan
- Damascus, in Syria
- Aleppo, also in Syria
- Jerusalem, claimed by both Palestine and Israel, is a city sacred to three religions, reflecting its age and ancient traditions
- Sidon, an ancient sea-port in the Lebanon
- Argos, one of the three oldest cities in Greece, in the north eastern Peloponnese
- Sikyon, 11 miles northwest of Corinth in the northern Peloponnese
- Athens, often referred to as the birthplace of modern civilisation.

UNINVITED COMPANIONS

Quite early in the development of human civilisation and society, religion became a central feature of everyday life: it rapidly embedded itself as the dominant principle of the great theocracies of Sumeria, Egypt, and Rome. From their beginnings in the covenant between God and the Hebrew Messiah, King David, the great Middle Eastern religions of Judaism, Christianity and Islam would eventually spread across the globe.

Have you ever considered how astonishing this is? How did religion ever survive the transition from a hunting society's belief in the spirits of the wild animals they hunted, those of the forests, streams and grasslands in which they were pursued and of the wind, rain, Earth, Sun and Moon, which affected every aspect of their lives?

My contention is that from very early on, virtually as soon as Homo sapiens began to spread across the planet, we acquired unseen and largely unsuspected psychic masters. Then, as now, these entities viewed us as nothing more nor less than some form of livestock, regulating and directing every aspect of mankind's social, technological, spiritual and political life. They 'inoculated' our ancestors with cults and religions, empowered shamen, priests, magicians and kings, and created for their own purposes the many facets of the supernatural that still puzzle and disturb us fifty thousand years later.

These entities may have evolved on Earth long before humans appeared, but it's my belief that they arrived here from space. As discussed above, the ultimate evolutionary destiny of any organism would be to obviate the need for any form of physical body. Scientists have absolutely no idea of the nature of sentience, intelligence or the life-force itself. What is it that changes at the moment of death? Do near-death experiences provide us with evidence that death is, as many religions contend, the departure of an individual's 'soul'? If you conduct an internet search for 'Weight loss at death caused by departure of soul' or something similar, you'll find:

UNINVITED COMPANIONS

- accounts by some very sincere investigators who document a 20g loss of mass soon after death
- others by researchers who have neglected many of the basic conventions of 'controlled experimentation' and failed to consider all the possible causes of such mass-loss
- a wealth of posts by humanists, sceptics and cynics who base their hostile interpretations on their own belief system

But, as mentioned above, science cannot fully explain the difference between a living individual and one who died peacefully in their sleep in terms of biochemistry alone. Nor can it account for the many astounding accounts of adults and even very young children who seem to recall previous existences in exact detail.

Let us assume that there is a 'life force' in all plants and animals: let's further assume that on planets billions of years older than the Earth, intelligent entities managed to avoid the baleful fate seemingly predicted by the Fermi Paradox and continue to evolve. Eventually they lost all dependence on aerobic respiration, the need to take in food and no longer required organs to carry out these functions. They evolved into clouds of pure thought energy, composed, perhaps, of exotic sub-atomic particles, 'strings' or combinations of interacting wave phenomena.

If this seems a little hard to swallow, it's worth recalling that electrons can behave as if they are either particles or waves in various circumstances and that photons at rest are considered to have **no mass at all**.

As Einstein demonstrated in his Special Theory of Relativity:

$$E = mc^2$$

(To put it simply, mass and energy are interchangeable) The kind of life-forms to which we are accustomed are basically very inefficient devices for

UNINVITED COMPANIONS

converting one into the other: it is surely naive to not at least acknowledge the possibility that other, better strategies may exist.

Our hypothetical energy beings must be capable of growth, self-replication and the absorption of external energy. Perhaps they move from star system to star system as bundles of waves at the speed of light (like a torch beam!) or perhaps they are capable of propelling themselves in some exotic way (A near mass-less object will eventually reach the speed of light if a beam of photons is projected from it in one direction!)

Quantum leap! I cannot pretend to have the skill with mathematics to prove these contentions or any of those I'm about to put before you: but sometimes it is entirely valid to make a proposition based on a logical review of the possibilities. As our old friend Sherlock Holmes from Chapter Five stated on more than one occasion:

". . . when you have eliminated the impossible, whatever remains, however improbable, must be the truth"

I think it very possible that our postulated energy beings can absorb energy directly from the medium through which they are travelling, in the form of electromagnetic radiation. Remember, **this is exactly what green plants do during photosynthesis!** They use the energy from sunlight, catalysed by the green pigment chlorophyll, to make sugar from carbon dioxide and water. (Just as well that they do: this reaction produces oxygen as a waste product, the origin of **all** the oxygen in our atmosphere, the molecules of water in the sea and most of the minerals in our world's crust and mantle!)

The next quantum leap: when these entities come across an inhabited world, they switch to what, I should imagine, is a more-easily assimilated energy source: the outpourings from active nervous systems. On some planets there might be slim pickings from lowly life-forms such as crustaceans or

UNINVITED COMPANIONS

molluscs. On others they might find highly evolved organisms with central nervous systems that are well on their way to developing intelligence. Just occasionally, they might get really lucky and find complex, sentient creatures like our ancestors and begin a long-term occupation.

Indulge me for a minute or two! Let's accept that at some time in the past our planet was chanced upon by a swarm of energy beings. They moved across the globe, 'feeding' on low-grade mental output, until they reached the Olduvai Gorge, The Ethiopian Highlands or wherever else human genesis began. At this point they recognised the potential of the shambling man-apes that were the progenitors of mankind. As our ancestors evolved and spread outwards across the planet, so did the 'visitors'.

A number of writers have suggested that human evolution and the development of human society may have been accelerated by outside influences. The mythologies of virtually every ancient society contain stories of how non-human entities brought to Earth the arts and sciences of agriculture, writing, tool making and house building. In the Egyptian pantheon, for example, the ibis-headed god Thoth gave the Egyptians magic and science, while Osiris introduced civilization and agriculture.

Perhaps the energy beings had a part to play in the development of our unique intelligence and incredibly rapid spread across the planet. It's possible that genetic 'tweaking' and a gradual exposure to areas of knowledge that would aid this process were their usual occupation strategy. The elite groups that ruled the human race then, and continue to do so now, may well have been the recipients of this arcane information.

The political theorist and writer David Icke is chiefly known for his suggestion that many of the ruling elite have genes acquired from ancient reptilian invaders from space. He claims that, even today, they are capable of morphing into 'reptilians' when under stress. I see much to admire in Icke's

UNINVITED COMPANIONS

research, particularly in regard to the methods used by the few to control the many, but I personally believe he may have overstated the reptilian thesis, to the detriment of wider credibility.

Nonetheless, like him, I can certainly see signs of a duality within the human population: this is most obvious in terms of the distribution of wealth and power. It is an astonishing yet true fact that, at the time of writing, 1% of the world's population controls over 50% of its wealth!

I don't intend developing this theme in the present work, but you might like to do your own research in these areas:

- How many separate organisations (or individuals) control global media? (TV, newspapers, social networks, etc.)

- Which schools and universities in the UK have generated the greatest number of religious, military, political and commercial leaders?

- Has *any* political system ever benefitted *all* of a nation's population? Or does all government ultimately just provide an opportunity for a ruling elite to line its pockets and entrench its position?

- Does the modern *state* educational system generally encourage children to ask questions, think laterally and develop a thirst for knowledge? Or does it attempt to indoctrinate and institutionalise them and turn them into increasingly unquestioning 'citizen consumers'?

- Are all advances in medicine available on demand to *every* member of the 'free' western democracies? Or does the ruling elite enjoy greater benefit, living longer and healthier lives?

- Did anyone ever vote to start a war? Why might you have been given a medal for shooting ten Germans on May 10th, 1944, but have been executed for carrying out the same action on May 10th, 1946?

UNINVITED COMPANIONS

- Why is it the default response of the political establishment to ridicule a belief in UFOs, ghosts, elementals, cryptids, and all other aspects of the paranormal, but continue to include leaders of mainstream religion in political decision making? (For example: the 26 'Lords Spiritual' in the House of Lords.)

Unless you at least **consider** the possibility that some of mankind's destiny has been – is – controlled by antipathetic non-human intelligences, it's pretty difficult to answer the points above.

But if we are to believe that these entities **do** share our world, how are they linked with the complete spectrum of paranormal phenomena?

My feeling is that the usual form of these energy beings is spherical: that their default appearance is the familiar opalescent shimmering orb. Accepting the thesis that these organisms are composed of some form of pure energy, I would suggest that, when necessary, one, or a group of them, although normally invisible to us, can manifest themselves into any shape or size they choose. By manipulation of their refractive index, the energy beings could appear transparent, translucent or completely solid. (From now on, if you don't mind, I'll use the initials EB for our putative companions.)

Suppose you were to accept an invitation to join me on a visit to Rendlesham Forest one night. The area already is, in my estimation, crowded with these psychic parasites: others pour in, attracted by our excitement and alert expectation. They start to enjoy a good 'feed' at our expense. Gradually, as the night wears on and we've neither seen nor heard anything unusual, and start to grow tired and lose enthusiasm. The EBs decide it's time to put on a show! A large green orb floats across the path in front of us. Above us, a triangle of coloured lights moves silently across the night sky. We hear footsteps crunching through the bracken at our side, yet no-one is visible. A large white stone thuds onto the sandy path in front of us: when you pick it up, it is warm.

UNINVITED COMPANIONS

Apported stone

We become wide awake again and super-sensitive to every noise and movement: our pulses race and our levels of excitement escalate rapidly. Then, on reviewing our digital cameras, a human-like figure appears on one image. Excitement immediately changes to fear: we turn and retreat from the Forest!

Linda and I have experienced *all* of these occurrences in the past (although not at the same time, I hasten to add!) The only explanation that appears to take them all into account is that they are different manifestations of *exactly* the same phenomenon.

In a similar sequence of events, EBs can gather anywhere and create a storm of human emotional response. These are a few, possibly familiar examples:

UNINVITED COMPANIONS

- In 1917 some EBs morph into a vision of the Virgin Mary on a hillside near Fatima, generating expectations and religious fervour that endure for centuries.

- In 1933 a cloud of energy coalesces into the shape of a huge water beast. It slithers across the road in front of Mr and Mrs Spicer as they drive alongside Loch Ness, beginning the modern wave of monster sightings

- An old man standing on a pier sees a giant dog by the light of his Tilley lamp and so convinces himself it is an omen of coming disaster that he dies soon after.

- The American pilot of a P-51 Mustang chases a glowing circle of light until he passes a safe altitude. His body is found later in the wreckage of his aircraft. The belief that 'Flying Saucers' are hostile craft from space soon spreads around the globe.

- A visitor to York finds himself watching a group of Roman Legionnaires marching silently through the darkened side street where he is standing.

- Two children see – and perhaps photograph – fairies, elves and goblins by a Yorkshire beck, starting a controversy that rages long after the girls' deaths.

A final thought: what might be the result of freeing ourselves from these hypothetical partners in evolution? The initial response might be that throwing off these age-old shackles could only be for the best: mankind would finally be free to control its own destiny. However, I have a feeling that the result might have a less than Utopian outcome.

William Golding's excellent book 'The Lord of the Flies' explores the results of the sudden removal of imposed order on a group of schoolboys

UNINVITED COMPANIONS

marooned on a remote island. Golding concludes that, without authority figures to impose order, the boys would rapidly revert to chaotic and destructive behaviour. You might also reflect on the descent into bloody civil war and inter-tribal aggression that seemed inevitably to follow the process of European decolonialisation in the 1940s, 50s and 60s. For example, India, under the moral leadership of Mahatma Mohandas K Ghandi, fought hard politically for half a century to free itself from the British Raj. As soon as independence was proclaimed, the country quickly descended into conflict between Hindus, Sikhs and Muslims that divided it into three states and resulted in the deaths of at least half a million people.

Perhaps if conclusive proof were ever found that we are the unwitting hosts of a myriad of superior alien intellects, the best thing might be to negotiate!

APPENDIX ONE

AROUND AND ABOUT IN RENDLESHAM FOREST

THROUGHOUT this book I have made frequent references to a location in coastal Suffolk, England called Rendlesham Forest. In December, 1980 it was the scene of possibly the most famous UFO encounter in the UK, when over several nights (the exact number is a little contentious!) a brightly-lit craft was allegedly witnessed moving through the forest, hovering over the nearby Bentwaters USAF base and shining laser-like beams onto 'hot row', a weapon storage facility at the base.

The fact that the weapons in question were most probably nuclear ordnance and that the witnesses to these events included numbers of security officers and the then Deputy Base Commander (a Lieutenant Colonel) lends the so-called Rendlesham Forest Incident (RFI) far more credibility than many similar accounts. (I should add that the assumption that military personnel and police offers are more reliable witnesses than, say, farmers or lorry drivers has always puzzled me! A police traffic officer actually has no more experience of the paranormal than anyone else. Of course, he should, in theory, have a reasonable understanding of the rules of evidence, but that's not true of a fighter pilot!)

UNINVITED COMPANIONS

Over the years since the RFI, many visitors have experienced the full range of paranormal phenomena while exploring the woods and nearby heathland. If we accept the conclusions I reached in the final chapter of this book, that is, perhaps, not too surprising.

Rendlesham Forest attracts scores of UFO enthusiasts, some of whom explore the woods at night. To me it seems highly possible that our energy beings consider this location almost as a picnic site! The out-pourings of alert expectation, excitement, nervousness and, at times, actual terror must be considerable.

Some visitors report 'traditional' UFOs: there are a few very credible videos, including a spectacular piece of footage obtained by authors and researchers John Hanson and Dawn Holloway.

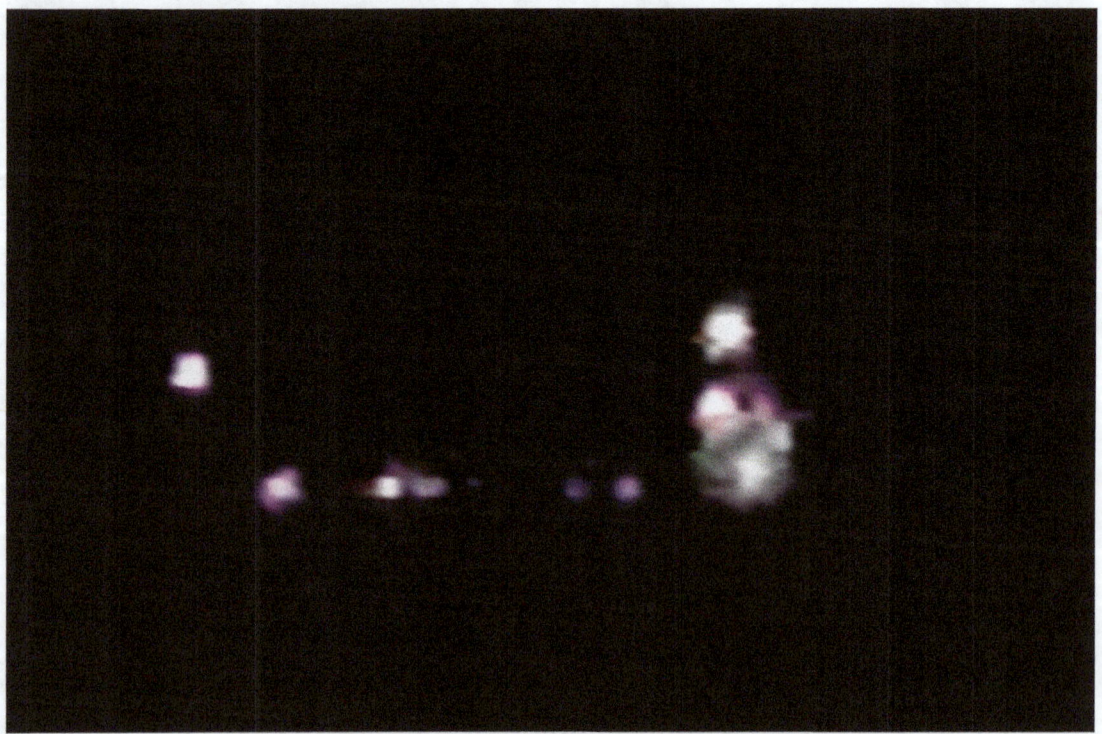

John Hanson & Dawn Holloway's Rendlesham Forest UFO

UNINVITED COMPANIONS

Other people exploring the trackways and field-margins of the forest have reported a wide range of other experiences:

- The most common phenomena are light-orbs, seen – and photographed – in a bewildering variety of sizes and colours.
- Swirling, dense mists are not infrequently encountered: these may form themselves into denser masses with the appearance of faces or humanoid figures.
- Coloured pin-points of light (which are definitely not flying insects) are often seen flitting through even the densest undergrowth.
- A number of regular visitors have reported encounters with a large Yeti-like creature as well as numerous black big cats: allegedly, these have even been seen in broad daylight.
- Unexplained falls of stones and other objects from the sky frequently occur: I myself have witnessed rounded, white pebbles arriving from above on two occasions. Another researcher witnessed a plastic elephant dropping onto the path in front of his group!
- Spatial disorientation and unexplained visions have often affected even the most level-headed walkers: here's an example.

Some dear friends of mine have long been very keen to buy a property in the Woodbridge area – they are fascinated by the events of December 1980 and visit Rendlesham Forest half a dozen times a year, despite it being a three-hour drive from their Sussex home. In July, 2011, they finally bought a very plush holiday retreat on a gated site on a beautiful slope overlooking the River Orwell.

One weekend, before they found their holiday home, the couple explored Rendlesham Forest several times, particularly the region between the famous East Gate and a Bronze Age Tumulus to the south. As they

UNINVITED COMPANIONS

walked along the path, they came across a **'... beautiful, quaint cottage, set back from the path in a well-kept garden'** (my friend's words.) They spent a while looking at it, discussing how ideal it would be to buy as their holiday home, before continuing along the path. Since my friends know the forest extremely well, they remarked to each other that it was strange they hadn't come across the property on previous visits...

That night, on returning home, they phoned me for a chat and spoke at length about the cottage. Linda and I were invited to the grand opening of their new home in August and took the opportunity to visit the forest: they were keen to show me the cottage and I was keen to visit the Tumulus, which

The Tumulus, Rendlesham Forest

I find to be a fascinating place. As we approached the location my friend remembered, he called out landmarks: finally he said **'It's here, round this corner...'** and then stopped in his tracks. He literally went white! Instead of the 'delapidated cottage' there stood a fairly ordinary pair of 1930s houses with a 'For Sale' sign.

UNINVITED COMPANIONS

Recovering his composure, my friend ran further along the path, calling out **'I remember these gates! This intersection was where we stood!'** and so on. Eventually he calmed down enough to give more details: apparently the 'footprint' of the cottage he'd seen was at right angles to that of the more modern building in front of us: its front wall was parallel to the trackway, not at ninety degrees as were the pair of semi-detached houses that now occupied the site.

Had my friends glimpsed a former property, long-since demolished? I have no idea, but I do definitely know that my big, tough mate was very shaken by the experience!

Encounters with 'ghosts' are reported a number of times a year, ranging from hooded monk-like figures to Second World War airmen.

UNINVITED COMPANIONS

Neither of these would be particularly out of place: the whole region is steeped in history, from the Anglo-Saxon burial site at Sutton Hoo, to the large tumulus on the southern boundary of the woods, to the numerous medieval priories in the Suffolk coastal strip. During World War 2, the Woodbridge base itself was equipped with the FIDO emergency landing system. As damaged RAF bombers approached over the North Sea, petrol-filled trenches either side of the main east-west runway were ignited. This allowed injured pilots to fly an easy straight-in approach even in foggy weather, but it also illuminated the base and silhouetted aircraft on finals. Many times, Luftwaffe night-fighters shot down aircraft just yards from safety.

If anyone reading this would like to investigate for themselves, the following map indicates the location of Rendlesham Forest and of its various supernatural 'hotspots'. Do bear in mind, however, that the Forest is a commercial enterprise, owned and maintained by the Forestry Commission for the production of softwoods. It's not unusual to find whole swathes of woodland cleared away, while others may be closed to visitors.

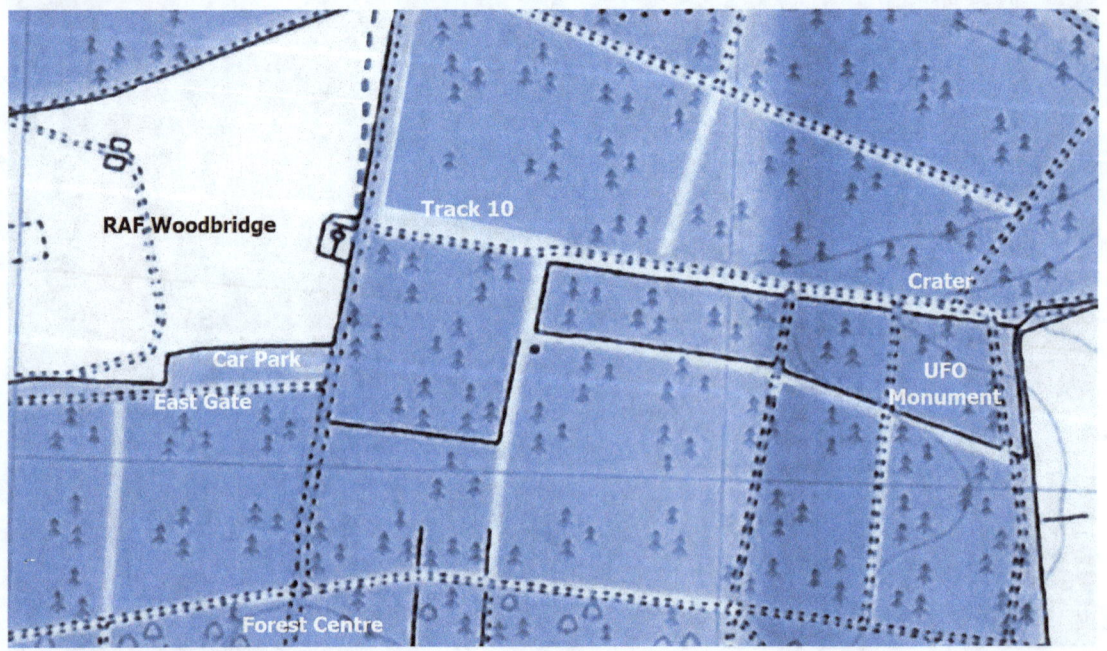

APPENDIX TWO

ABDUCTIONS IN THEORY AND PRACTICE

TWO of the most contentious areas in modern phenomenology are those of *alien contact* and *alien abduction*.

Arguably, communication with the apparent occupants of UFOs is as old as the history of the phenomenon itself. Some authors have claimed that Ezekiel's Old Testament meeting with four strange beings and their 'wheel within a wheel' is just such a Close Encounter of the Third Kind. The best-known and most influential contactee of the modern era is George Adamski.

This Polish-American amateur astronomer wrote three best-selling books about his alleged encounters with nordic-looking entities and his journeys to other planets with them: *Flying Saucers Have Landed* (1953), *Inside the Space Ships* (1955) and *Flying Saucers Farewell* (1961).

Numerous other well-discussed contact events occurred during the twentieth century, many of which are dismissed (even by UFOlogists) as self delusional or mischievous hoaxes: this is particularly true of those where intellectually challenged individuals claim to have travelled to other worlds or to be in possession of an 'important message for mankind'. Quite frequently the alien entities are described as tall, good-looking with long

UNINVITED COMPANIONS

blond hair and who often cannot wait to have sex with a seventy-year old car mechanic or similar!

Following the release of the excellent film *'Close Encounters of the Third Kind'* in 1977, tales of alien contact reportedly escalated dramatically: it is this effect (which occurs after most such films) that is seen by many psychologists as an example of 'the thought becoming the word'. Many of us, it appears seemingly wish to have participated in or have witnessed noteworthy events. A couple of examples of this are President Ronald Reagan claiming in a speech that he had taken part in the D-Day landings, when he was actually on a film lot in Hollywood at the time, and the number of London Eastenders who claim to have attended Violet Kray's funeral!

There may be another factor, which I'll consider at the end of this appendix!

In its presently-understood form abduction was first brought to the attention of the public – and the media – by the experiences of Betty and Barney Hill, which were recounted in John G Fuller's book, *'The Interrupted Journey'*. Driving back from a holiday at Niagara Falls to their home in Portsmouth in September, 1961, the Hills claimed to have witnessed a UFO and eight or more of its occupants (which would now be described as typical 'grey' types) Having stopped the car on two occasions, obtaining a closer look both of the UFO and its humanoid crew, the Hills drove away at speed. Following a cat-and-mouse pursuit, during which the couple experienced all kinds of vibrations and tingling sensations, they seemed to enter some form of trance-like state. When they returned to full consciousness, they found they had travelled 35 miles with no memory of having done so. A fortnight later, the Hills reported the incident to the US Air Force and details of their experience were recorded.

Over the next few years, following many vivid dreams and a gradual

UNINVITED COMPANIONS

increased recall of the event, Barney and Betty underwent hypnosis, during which further details of the craft and its occupants emerged.

The Hills' story has featured in numerous films and TV dramas.

A second high-profile account emerged in 1975, when the American logger, Travis Walton, was allegedly seen being taken aboard an alien craft. Walton had left the truck in which he had been travelling with his logging crew to investigate a bright light by the side of the road: as he approached the object, he was struck by a beam of light and thrown to the ground. His workmates turned and fled the scene, but one, Jerome Clark, claimed that, looking back over his shoulder, he observed Walton being illuminated by blue-green light, before rising backwards from the ground.

A couple of hours later another member of the crew, Ken Peterson, phoned local police to report that Walton was missing, triggering a five-day search that concluded abruptly when Walton reappeared. Confused and disoriented, the logger reported patchy memories of entering the UFO and being subjected to various procedures by its occupants.

The whole case (which was the subject of a 1993 Paramount Pictures film entitled *'Fire in the Sky'*) has been the subject of much controversy ever since. This chiefly centres around the reliability of the many polygraph ('lie detector') tests taken by Walton and several other members of the logging team over the years, some of which were passed, some failed, with others being inconclusive. Some researchers have challenged the dependability of the testing carried out at the time, and it is the case that Walton has passed all subsequent polygraph examinations performed with modern, more credible equipment.

Many similar 'close encounters of the fourth kind' have since been reported, some more believable than others. In fact, some investigators claim as many as three and a half *million* Americans have been abducted!

UNINVITED COMPANIONS

A casual skim through the accounts of some of these abductees might quickly lead you to conclude that they can be classified as:

- **Wishful thinkers:** people with a deep interest in the UFO phenomenon who are predisposed to interpret an odd experience of their own as an abduction.

- **Attention seekers:** individuals whose claims are based upon their desire for 'five minutes of fame.' These often seem to be people with low self-esteem, who are frequently unemployed or in low-paid jobs.

- **Opportunists:** would-be authors and lecturers who invent or exaggerate their experiences in order to give their careers a boost.

- **The intellectually challenged:** a group containing suggestible and emotionally vulnerable individuals who are exploited by others for their own purposes.

You've probably already guessed that Linda and I have had an experience with some of the characteristics of an abduction: you may like to consider which of the above categories we fit into!

One Sunday night in October 2011, Linda and I were driving home from a meteorite show in London. As we left the A11 and turned onto the A47 that loops eastwards to the south of Norwich, we chatted quietly, reflecting on our unexpectedly uneventful journey on some of the busiest roads in the UK. I remarked that the satnav was predicting our ETA for exactly nine o' clock, ten minutes having been shaved off by the light traffic we'd encountered. We decided we should turn off the A47 into the village of Brundall and buy a Chinese take-away, it being a little late to start cooking.

I should explain that there is just a single roundabout between our joining the A47 and the turn off to the tiny village where we live: it is brightly-lit

UNINVITED COMPANIONS

with a garage and McDonald's drive-in, and hardly something you could miss: in fact, it is nearly always necessary to come to a halt and wait for a gap in the traffic from the right. And yet on this night Linda suddenly exclaimed:

"You've gone past our turning!"

I replied that we couldn't have done: we hadn't reached the roundabout yet. The previously clear and starry night suddenly seemed darker, with an intense blackness to the sky. I slowed down to look for familiar landmarks: sure enough, we were a mile past our turning! Glancing at the satnav, I was astonished to see that the predicted arrival time was now 9.10!

What had happened during the missing ten minutes? We have no idea!

I make absolutely no claims about this event: there were certainly no signs that we'd been probed or implanted (I think I'd have remembered that!) and we didn't see any strange objects in the sky. Some might say we were tired and at the end of a long, familiar journey, but, as I mentioned above, we were anticipating turning off our route at the roundabout and were not particularly fatigued because of the easy journey we'd had.

Of course, I'm biased because this is my book, but I feel that the **Energy Being** argument works really well in explaining both the contactee and abductee phenomena. Once again, we have a situation where a few hundred apparently plausible accounts spawn literally millions more around the world in a short space of time. Once again, because of the frisson of excitement, expectation and perhaps even fear that the stories engender, continued psychic outpourings occur: three and a half million Americans constantly fearful of further alien abduction would provide plenty of nourishment for their invisible and uninvited companions!

UNINVITED COMPANIONS

Photograph of a supposedly-extinct Thylacine

APPENDIX THREE

A CIRCULAR ARGUMENT!

PROBABLY nothing divides opinion within the 'paranormal community' more than the increasingly complex designs of flattened plants that started to appear in West Country crop fields in the middle of the twentieth century. British TV companies seem to operate under instructions to make programmes that explain or debunk *any* unusual occurrence, even those that are not widely seen as having paranormal origins. A recent example was an hour-long TV documentary about rotating ice circles that are occasionally discovered in freezing rivers. I have *never* met anyone who thought these were anything other than natural phenomena, but the presenter continually alluded to alleged beliefs in a supernatural genesis for the discs.

Although there are earlier reports (including one by Sir Patrick Moore in 1963!) the great majority of crop formations have occurred from the end of the seventies until the present day. Two practical jokers, Doug Bower and Dave Chorley, claim to have constructed many of the original designs using ropes and planks, and it is undeniable that there are many individuals and groups who have publically demonstrated the ability to replicate even the most elaborate designs. Nevertheless, there are plenty of people who maintain a belief in a paranormal or extraterrestrial origin for at least some

UNINVITED COMPANIONS

crop circles and who spend many weekends each summer investigating and cataloguing new structures as they appear.

Since crop circles are most frequently found in fields of wheat or barley, researchers are generally known as **Cereologists** (Or, more correctly, Cerealogists.) Most of them freely acknowledge that many structures are man-made, these days often incorporating advertising logos or slogans for financial gain. But many of the more extraordinary crop designs seem to have appeared too abruptly and to be too perfect to have been the work of humans, even if they were armed with satnavs and laser pointers.

The amusing TV program 'QI' once commissioned an organisation called 'Circlemakers', founded by artists Rod Dickinson and John Lundberg, to reproduce its logo in a field of oilseed rape, thus 'proving' that all crop circles have a similar origin. As much as I admire Stephen Fry's intellect and wit, here I think he was guilty of an undistributed premise, along the lines of:

"A lemon is a yellow fruit, therefore all yellow fruits are lemons"

The crop circle edition of QI (which aired in the eighth series of the show) allowed Mr Fry to display his usual cynical view of the supernatural and occult. It would be interesting to know how these deeply-entrenched opinions came to be formed and whether he will retain them on his deathbed!

The usual arguments for a mundane origin for crop circles are:

- Most formations are found in easily accessible areas where the makers could slip in and out without detection
- Many elaborate designs have been replicated by groups of debunkers
- No-one has witnessed a crop circle forming spontaneously

UNINVITED COMPANIONS

- The majority are found in regions with occult or spiritual connections (eg. Near Stonehenge, Avebury etc) and were constructed there to guarantee a receptive audience.

Although some of these arguments are illogical or, well, **circular**, it remains the case that no reliable accounts of crop circle formation exist: or, at least, any that didn't involve human beings. To nail my colours to the mast, I personally feel that the modern wave of complex designs have predominantly mischievous, commercial or intentionally misleading origins. However, I also accept the possibility that some of the **oldest** records may refer to a genuinely paranormal phenomenon.

What interests me more than **who** is responsible for modern crop circles, is **why** they felt inspired to make them! While it may well be true that, after a few beers, Doug and Dave decided to wander away from the pub and spend a couple of hours tramping down the wheat on a nearby farm, you have to wonder what on Earth gave them the idea of doing so? Again, the Energy Being postulate fits well here: an original phenomenon – either natural or supernatural – causes increasing interest.

UNINVITED COMPANIONS

EBs inspire individuals or groups of humans to produce increasingly elaborate and apparently significant designs. This, as we have seen, generates two decades or more of argument, excitement and anticipation (and presumably fear of being caught by a farmer!)

APPENDIX FOUR

CAN ENERGY BEINGS CONTROL OUR BEHAVIOUR?

A SEARCH through the media reveals the surprising frequency with which criminals offer as an explanation of their actions that:

"The voices in my head told me to do it!"

Psychologists generally identify this statement as evidence of schizophrenia, but (as every parent will know!) a variation of it is also a common excuse used by children. One of my own daughters had, like many youngsters, an 'imaginary playmate' whom she would frequently blame for an incidence of poor behaviour or minor damage around the home. When 'the voices' are given as the rationale for locking your sister in the garage, that can almost be amusing: when they provide the authority for shooting your classmates or murdering prostitutes it's a little more serious!

In his 1976 book, **'The Origin of Consciousness in the Breakdown of the Bicameral Mind',** American psychologist Julian Jaynes advanced the intriguing theory that our distant ancestors (before around 1000 BC) did not have the conscious mind of modern humans. He suggested that their general actions were regulated by habit or conditioned response, in much the same way as animals. When a new, perhaps stressful situation arose, the

UNINVITED COMPANIONS

right temporal cortex of the brain generated auditory verbal hallucinations (voices!) that provided suggestions for alternative actions. These, Jaynes believed, were interpreted as communications from ancestors or gods and unquestioningly obeyed. (Herein, of course, lie the origins of religion, spirituality and mythology!)

Jaynes concluded that consciousness (linguistic meta-cognition) replaced this bicameral dialogue as human society became more complex and other inputs such as writing and codified laws were developed. He also suggested that varying degrees of our ancient bicameralism still exist in some modern humans.

I've never been **told** that I'm schizophrenic, but I must admit that I do occasionally enter into a mental dialogue with myself, particularly during decision making:

"Shall I have another glass of wine? Hmmm . . . I do need to lose a bit of weight . . . Oh: go on then!"

I'm pretty confident most of us do this: but it's a part of our normal thinking: having no-one else to help with the decision-making process, we review the pros and cons with ourselves! The difference between this behaviour, Jaynes' bicameral theory and some aspects of clinical schizophrenia is that I know it's **me** giving **myself** advice and am ready to accept responsibility for any resulting actions.

Interestingly, Jaynes' theories have been linked to the discovery that applying a small electric shock to the right side of the brain can induce visual as well as auditory hallucinations. This, some claim, could be a mechanism by which people with vestigial bicameralism might come to believe they have seen a ghost or other paranormal object.

You can probably see where I'm heading with this! I would contend that

UNINVITED COMPANIONS

the phenomena of bicameralism and of 'voices in the head' might actually originate in a person's partial awareness that an external intelligence – an energy being – is attempting to initiate an action that would generate a burst of psychic activity. Just imagine how much fear, anxiety and anger was caused by the apparently random killing of five prostitutes by Jack the Ripper in east London in 1888, or when 16-year-old Brenda Spencer shot and killed two people and wounded eight more at Grover Cleveland Elementary School, California. When asked why she had done it, Spencer reportedly replied: *"I don't like Mondays!"*

If we were ever able to prove with absolute certainty that the 'Uninvited Companions' that constitute the central thesis of this book actually exist, it would give an entirely new direction to our understanding of aberrant behaviour. It's quite likely that the very earliest hominids exercised little or no restraint: the social life of Chimpanzees can be appallingly violent and Bonobos seem to be the most sexually-obsessed mammals on the planet! What makes us different is that most of us, most of the time display **social altruism**: we subordinate our needs, urges and desires in order to benefit the group of which we are part. This is the reason most of us intuitively find murder, violence, paedophilia and theft totally abhorrent. It's also why such acts fill us with horror and disbelief: on hearing about the latest atrocities in the Middle East, we might find ourselves asking *"How could anyone do such things?"*

Perhaps the Energy Being theory, if not a defence, is, in some cases at least, a partial explanation.

UNINVITED COMPANIONS

APPENDIX FIVE

"PLAY UP! PLAY UP! AND PLAY THE GAME!"

I'M sure it must have occurred to most people that sport and warfare are two sides of the same coin: both are essentially tribal, competitive and engender powerful emotions in participants and spectators alike. In fact the gladiatorial spectacles of the Roman Empire blur the lines to the extent that they become virtually indiscernible!

The title of this section is taken from the poem "Vitaï Lampada", written by Henry John Newbolt in 1892. The poem contends that the values learned on the cricket pitches of British public schools were a major factor in the victorious campaigns of the British Empire's armies. This thought is echoed by the famous quote attributed (probably wrongly!) to the Duke of Wellington: "The Battle of Waterloo was won on the playing-fields of Eton". There can be little doubt that the concepts of team spirit, striving for the greater good, shrugging off fatigue and pain to achieve the ultimate goal *for no personal reward* are all emphasised in the teaching of sport at public school.

As a young man in the late 60s I attended Dartmouth Royal Naval College and can confirm that team-building through competitive sport was very much

UNINVITED COMPANIONS

part of the officer training programme. The various 'Divisions' at Dartmouth (I was in Cunningham!) were pitted against each other in a full range of sports and other activities, and non-participants were expected to support their Division enthusiastically from the sidelines.

A similarly curious relic of British Culture is witnessed on the Thames every spring, when teams from Oxford and Cambridge compete in the University Boat Race. What this has to do with the majority of us is beyond my understanding: true, my elder brother rowed for his college (Peterhouse) and true, I've been made welcome as a guest-lecturer at the Institute of Astronomy in Cambridge, but neither of these factors explain why I feel disappointed when the Dark Blues of Oxford beat the Light Blues of Cambridge!

This is also the case in the modern version of Formula 1 motor racing. How normal working people are induced to take an interest in the spectacle of a bunch of multi-millionaires driving in a procession around a circuit, before three of them spray each other with £500 bottles of Champagne, is one of life's real mysteries! (I should say: I never miss a televised Grand Prix!)

I should imagine that Henry Newbold would be appalled to witness the behaviour of some modern-day sportsmen, and even more so of some of their 'fans'. Consider, for a moment, professional football: there doesn't seem to be much evidence of 'team spirit, striving for the greater good, shrugging off fatigue and pain to achieve the ultimate goal **for no personal reward'** in the actions of many of today's players!

And yet, the modern game draws huge crowds from all areas of society, united in a fervent support of 'their team'. Curiously, it doesn't seem to matter whether or not the team they support plays near their home or where they were born: Manchester United and Chelsea have massive followings from all around the world!

UNINVITED COMPANIONS

An even stranger fact is that teams in the English Premier League are predominantly made up of foreign players: at the time of writing, 67% of playing time was by overseas footballers. What's more, over half of the team managers were foreign: so, what exactly are fans being loyal *to*? Well: to a brand: a product!

This situation pretty much pervades all modern sport: even the one-time bastions of amateur endeavour, Rugby Union and Athletics, now welcome overseas players and reward success with massive pay-checks. Competitive sport has become a truly global phenomenon!

This is only a suggestion: but what if our uninvited companions, the Energy Beings, realised sometime around 1919 that warfare, while generating plenty of the psychic output they needed to thrive, was ultimately becoming counterproductive. The introduction of machine guns, tanks, aircraft and increasingly energetic explosives meant that warfare quickly became *too* efficient a way of killing people. This was, perhaps, underlined by the excesses of World War 2 and the advent of thermonuclear bombs. Our parasitic masters may suddenly have realised that global warfare had acquired the potential to wipe the human race – and them – from the face of the planet! Perhaps the suggestion was made to the ruling elite: wars were to be kept small and manageable, while the necessary extra psychic output would be provided through a logarithmic growth of the importance of sport.

During my time in education, I've seen a total sea-change in the aspirations of secondary school students: where once they might be persuaded to work really hard to gain a university place to study languages, medicine, engineering and so on, a fair percentage of Year 10 students, when asked what they hoped to do after leaving school, frequently replied that they were going to be footballers or sing in a girl/boy band. These are ambitions that would probably suit our hypothetical companions admirably,

UNINVITED COMPANIONS

since both are productive areas for high output of emotional and psychic energy (unlike Science, where growing numbers of trained minds might begin to ferment awkward questions!).

APPENDIX SIX

IMAGES OF THE PARANORMAL

IN this section are a few genuine photographs taken in Rendlesham Forest by my wife Linda and me on various occasions between 2010 and 2015. They show a range of orbs of different sizes, colours and textures, some of which were visible at the time: others were only discovered when the camera's data was viewed on a computer when we returned home.

The only enhancements made were adjustments to contrast and 'gamma' levels, which were carried out using 'IrfanView' freeware.

Here is an example: these Herons were photographed at dusk, resulting in a somewhat dark picture. The 'after' image has had both contrast and gamma increased to reveal more detail of the birds.

The 'snow pair' were taken as an experiment in our garden: we took a series of photographs, before Linda tried the whistling technique. The next image includes an apparent orb!

We make no extravagant claims for any of the pictures, but I have added our interpretation of them.

UNINVITED COMPANIONS

'Snow Pair' and (below) Opalescent orb

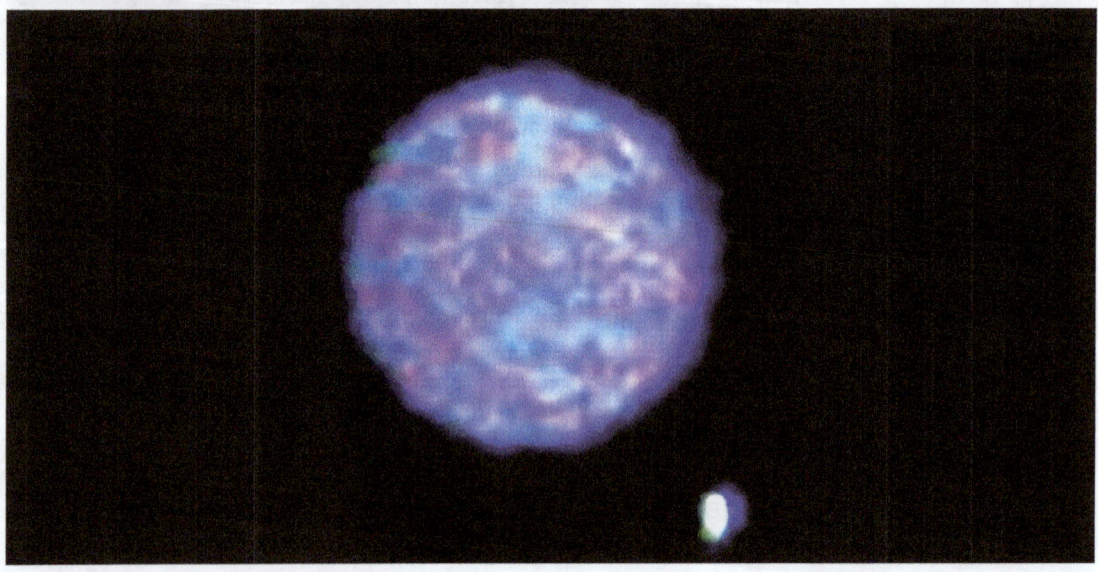

UNINVITED COMPANIONS

(Above) Green orb

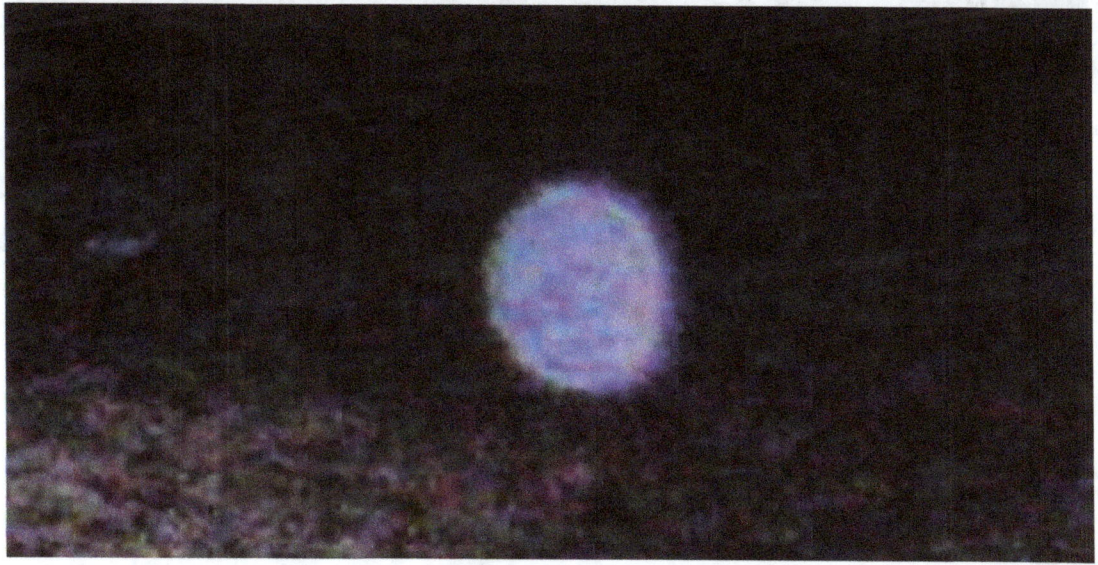

UNINVITED COMPANIONS

UNINVITED COMPANIONS

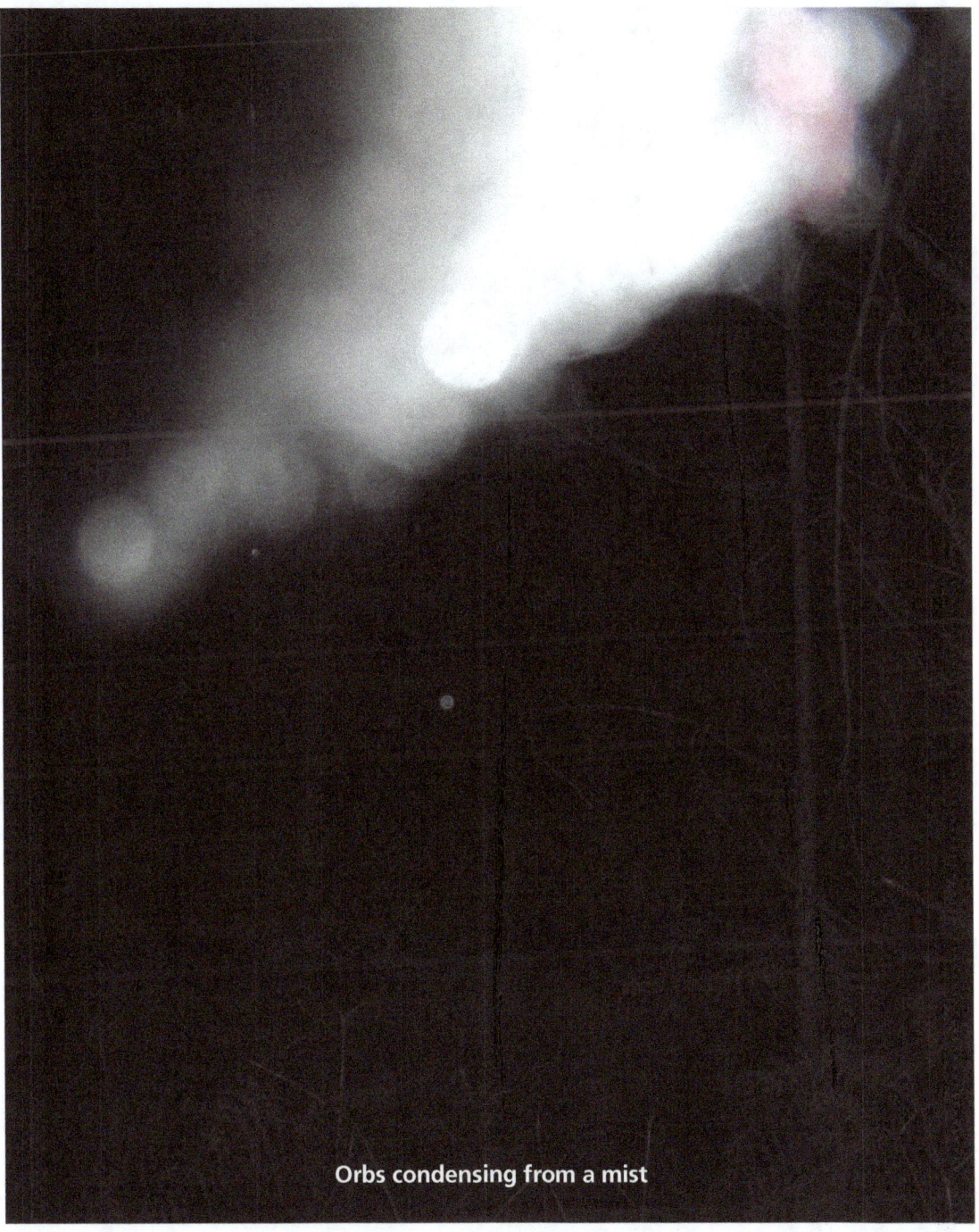

Orbs condensing from a mist

UNINVITED COMPANIONS

Orbs of a variety of colours

50cm orb seen and photographed in Rendlesham Forest

UNINVITED COMPANIONS

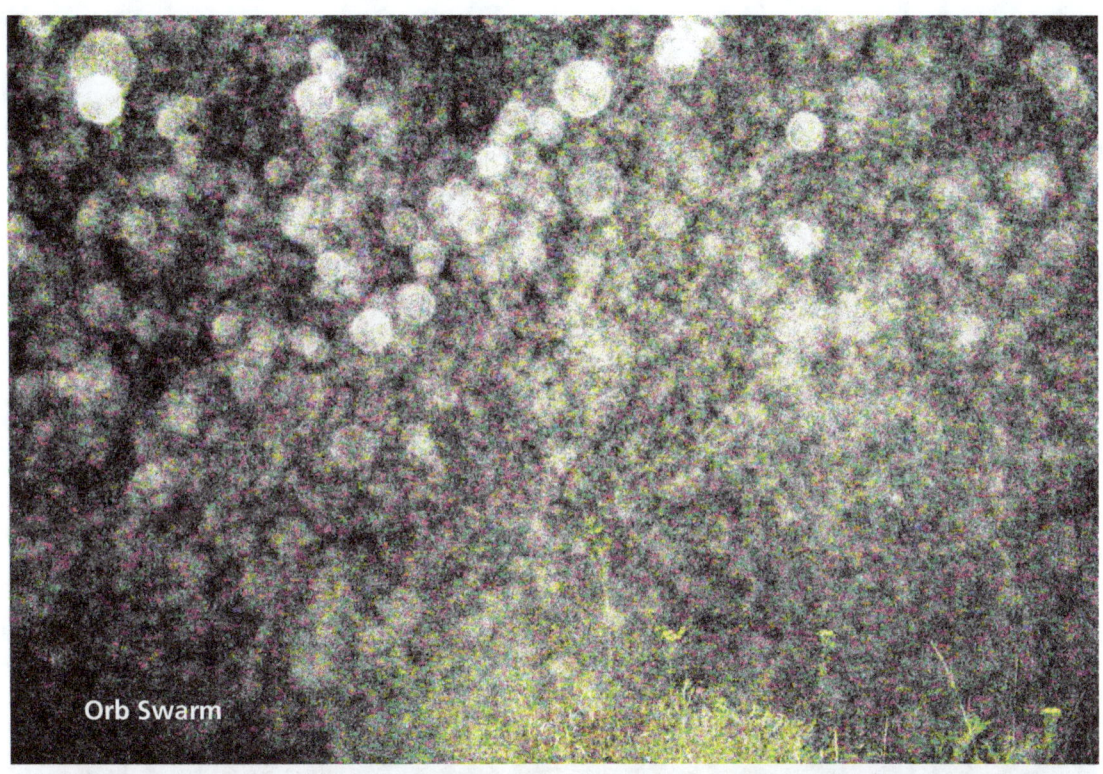

Orb Swarm

Blue orb with internal structure

UNINVITED COMPANIONS

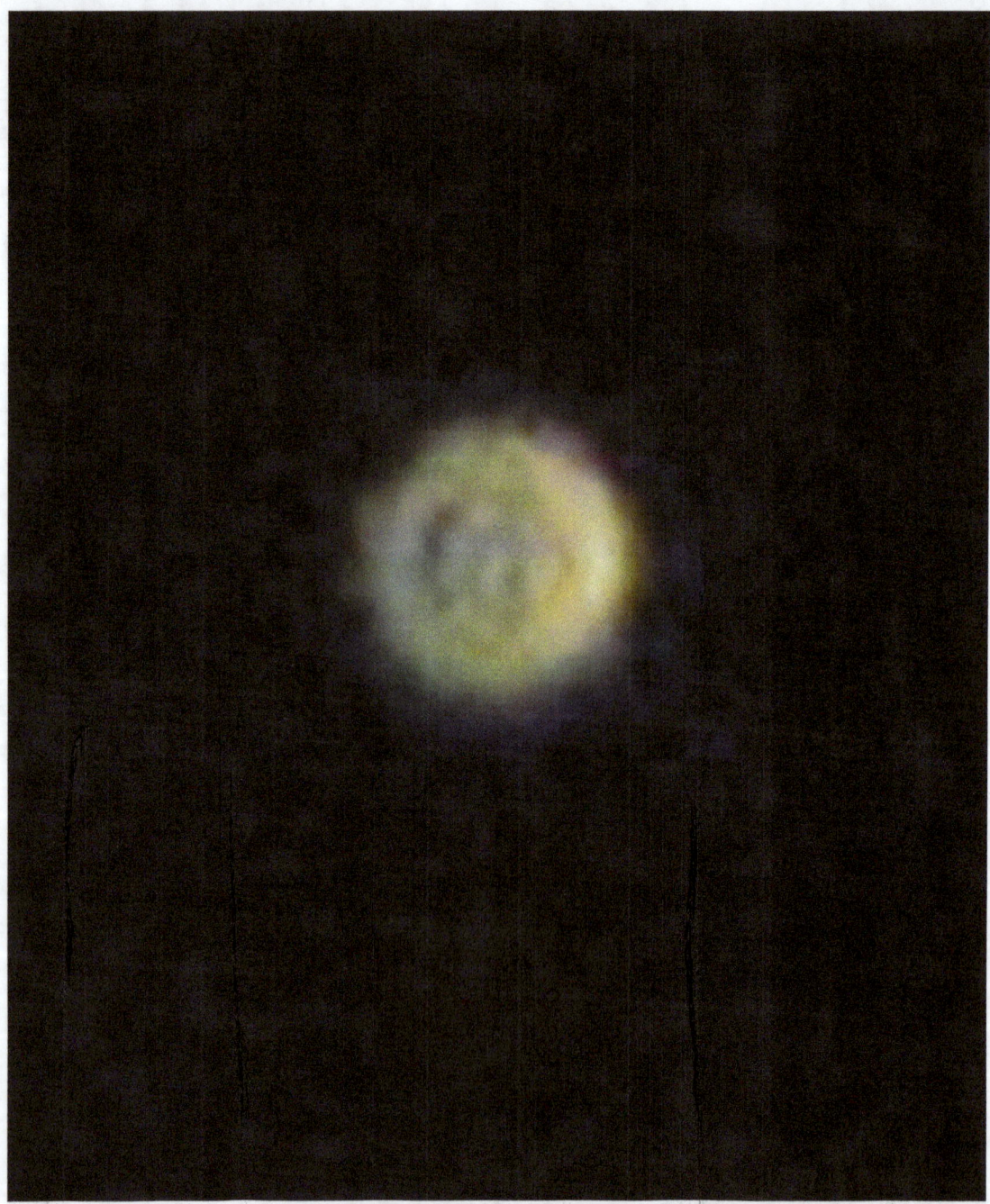

The 'Werthers' orb

Glossary

Abduction

A relatively modern phenomenon when a human being is taken aboard an alien craft against their will, often for intrusive physical examination.

Altruism

Putting the needs of others above one's own with no thought of reward.

Blitz

From the German word for 'lightning', the original meaning at the start of WW2 was a rapid attack that took defenders by surprise. Later, it was used for the carpet bombing of Britain's industry and centres of population

Boffin

Another piece of WW2 slang: it is an affectionate term for a scientist collaborating with one of the armed forces. The origin is not known, but there are characters with the surname 'Boffin' in books by Dickens, Morris and Tolkien.

CGI

An acronym for Computer Generated Imagery: any piece of graphics, video or pictorial design generated using a computer.

UNINVITED COMPANIONS

Close Encounter
The scientist and UFOlogist J. Allen Hynek devised a three-level scale to describe the various types of interaction between humans and the UFO phenomenon:

Close Encounter of the 1st Kind
Visual sighting of a UFO at a range closer than 500 feet

Close Encounter of the 2nd Kind
Physical interaction with a UFO (Electrical equipment malfunctioning, car engines stopping, detection by radar etc)

Close Encounter of the 3rd Kind
Interaction with apparent extraterrestrials or other occupants of a UFO

Other researchers have added up to four further levels and numerous sub-sets. The expression became popular after the 1977 Spielberg film.

Contactee
A UFO witness who claims to have interacted with an EBE, either communicating in person telepathically, using sign language or normal speech, or remotely in some way.

Continental drift
The movement of tectonic plates with respect to each other that has created the shapes of the Earth's continents. The process was hypothesised by Alfred Wegener in 1912, but dismissed until research during International Geophysical Year in 1957 provided confirmatory evidence.

Cryptid
An organism (animal or plant) whose existence has not been confirmed by science

UNINVITED COMPANIONS

Cryptozoology
The study of cryptid animals (For example: the Yeti, Sea Serpent and Chupacabra)

Digicam
A camera that stores images digitally on a memory card or drive, as opposed to on film, obviating the requirement for lengthy and expense processing

EBE
An acronym for 'extra-terrestrial biological entity', a commonly-used expression for living occupants of UFOs (As opposed to robotic operators)

Elementals
Although originally associated with the four elements of Earth, Fire, Air and Water, nowadays the term is employed more widely to include a wide variety of supernatural spirits.

EMF meter
Electromagnetic Field Meters are extensively used by paranormal investigators to detect changes in ambient EM fields allegedly caused by spirits.

Father Ted
An original and highly entertaining sitcom about three Irish priests and their housekeeper. It attained cult status and ran for three series from 1995 – 1998.

Great Glen
Scotland is divided from south-west to north-east by a transverse slip fault. The deep valley formed by movement of this fault is water-filled for much of its length and includes Lochs Ness, Oich, Lochy and Linnhe.

UNINVITED COMPANIONS

Hippie (also 'Hippy')

The hippie movement was a youth sub-culture that spread across the western world from the west coast of America. Although with hindsight the whole lifestyle looks naive, impractical and inextricably associated with music, eastern culture and drugs, it did bring about the emancipation of the youth of the USA and western Europe.

Jack Kerouac

American 'beat' poet, Kerouac, together with Alan Ginsberg and William Burroughs, is considered a progenitor of the hippie movement. His iconoclastic writings inspired a generation to question traditional values and rebel against proscriptive authority.

Meteoritics

This is the scientific study of meteorites: their classification, structure, chemical composition and origins. It's the area in which I earn a living!

Paranormal

That which is outside or beyond the normal

Science Fiction

SF is a genre of literature (and recently film) that combines narrative with scientific realities, possibilities or hypotheses. The earliest examples date back as far as ancient Greece and China, but in its modern form SF is generally agreed to have emerged at the end of the nineteenth century, flourishing in the forties, fifties and sixties.,

SD card

This stands for 'secure digital card' and is the name given to compact storage devices that slot into phones, cameras, satnavs etc.

UNINVITED COMPANIONS

Spliff
A term used by some for a cigarette containing the drug marijuana.

Translucent
This term is used for materials that allows light to pass through, but which scatter or distort it during the process.

Warminster
A town in Wiltshire which achieved notoriety in the 1960s when many witnesses claimed to have observed UFOs (Especially over or near Cradle Hill)

Welsh Triangle
This region of West Wales around Broadhaven was the alleged scene of a number of mysterious UFO-related occurrences in the 1970s. These included a giant 'spaceman' seen by local people peering into their cottage windows and a classic UFO observed by staff and pupils of a primary school.

UNINVITED COMPANIONS

Dr Edgar Mitchell seen here sharing a moment with our author David Bryant

BIBLIOGRAPHY

Some books I have enjoyed!

Bernard Heuvelmans: *'On the Track of Unknown Animals'*
Bernard Heuvelmans: *''In the wake of the Sea Serpent'*,
Nicholas Witchell: *'The Loch Ness Story'*
George Adamski: *'Inside the Space Ships*
Julian Jaynes: *'The Origin of Consciousness in the Breakdown of the Bicameral Mind'*
Brenda Butler, Jenny Randles and Dot Street: *'Sky Crash'*
J Allen Hynek: *'The Hynek UFO Report'*
Fuller, John G.: *'Interrupted Journey'*
Travis Walton: *'The Walton Experience'*
Richard Dawkins: *'The God Delusion'*
Carl Sagan: *'Cosmos'*
Andrew Zimmerman Jones with Daniel Robbins: *'String Theory For Dummies'*
Stephen Hawking: *'A brief History of Time'*
Ivan T Sanderson: *'Things'*
Brian Sykes: *'The Nature of the Beast'*

UNINVITED COMPANIONS

David Bryant with UFO researcher and author Nick Pope,
MoD Air Desk Sec (AS) 2A 1991-94

A 'shadow figure' captured in Rendlesham Forest

UNINVITED COMPANIONS

Photo credits

All photos are by the author, except:

Plate 1, page 15	Terry Maloney
Plate 10, page 47	Unknown, Public Domain
Plate 11, page 50	The Boy's Standard, Public Domain
Plate 12, page 55	Arthur Wright, Public Domain
Plate 14, page 59	Philip Burne-Jones, Public Domain
Plate 15, page 62	Unknown, Public Domain
Plate 19, page 89	Abraham Fleming, Public Domain
Plate 20, page 95	Public domain
Plate 22, page 122	John Hanson
Plate 24, page 135	Unknown, Public Domain
Plate 26, page 140	Unknown, Public Domain

DISCLAIMER

All material in this book, including text and images, is protected by copyright and this is owned by David Bryant of 'The Space Station' unless credited otherwise. It may not be copied, reproduced or republished in any way without the copyright owner's consent, except for personal, non-commercial use.

The majority of the photographs in this book were taken by the author: credit for the remainder is given where possible. In a few cases, despite diligent searches, it has not been possible to locate the original source of an image: these are, however, all identified as being in the public domain. Should one of these be subject to copyright, please contact the publisher so the matter can be rectified.

SPACEROCKS UK

DAVID BRYANT, BSc, Cert Ed is the only full-time meteorite dealer in England. His company 'Spacerocks UK' holds a complete inventory of all meteorite types, from 4.5 billion year old common chondrites, to iron meteorites, rare and beautiful pallasites and even pieces of the Moon, Mars and the Asteroid Vesta!

He is a member of the IMCA, (International Meteorite Collectors Association) and all his items are sold with an A4 factsheet and guarantee of authenticity. David has delivered lectures about meteorites at meetings of the British Astronomical Association, the Society for Popular Astronomy, for the BBC's 'Stargazing Live' events and astronomical societies all over the country.

David sells his meteorites at rock and mineral shows around the UK, from Cambridgeshire to Devon and at most of his public lectures.

All these items can be purchased by 'phone, **01603 715933** or from the **SPACEROCKS UK** website at:

http://www.spacerocksuk.com
email: info@spacerocksuk.com

His wife, Linda, makes a wide range of beautiful meteorite and impactite jewellery using solid silver chains and findings, which are available from her website:

http://www.space-jewellery.co.uk

David and Linda Bryant seen here recently, displaying items available for purchase at one of the Spacerocks UK stalls

OUR FORBIDDEN MOON

By David Bryant (Foreword by Nick Pope)

136 pages, some in colour

David Bryant's book *Our Forbidden Moon* has taken fifteen years of meticulous planning and research to write. During encounters with over thirty astronauts and cosmonauts, including seven of the twelve alleged Moonwalkers, the author gradually became aware of a number of major inconsistencies in their recollections of the Apollo program. Furthermore, in occasional unguarded moments, several space travellers have revealed personal experiences of the UFO phenomenon and hinted at even more dramatic events. *Our Forbidden Moon* examines these revelations and considers whether there might be a link between UFOs, extraterrestrial races and mankind's forty-year failure to travel beyond low Earth orbit. The author uses his knowledge gained during forty years as a teacher, lecturer and respected authority on spaceflight and meteoritics to ask controversial questions and provide convincing solutions.

DANGER FROM THE SKIES

By David Bryant *(Foreword by Dr Rob Bryant)*

132 pages, some in colour

Does Mankind's nemesis lurk out in deep space, beyond the edge of the Solar System?

Danger From The Skies offers a completely new 'spin' on the effect of major impact events on the evolution of life on Earth and the objects that caused them. Darwinian theory alone cannot adequately explain the sudden disappearance of highly successful groups such as the trilobites, dinosaurs and giant Pleistocene mammals: what factor is missing from the textbooks? With a background in Biological Sciences and Astronomy and as the UK's only full-time meteorite dealer, author David Bryant has reached some startling and novel conclusions about the causes of mass extinctions. The book examines the evidence for past planet-shattering impacts and discusses what – if anything – can be done to prevent such an event in the future.